Face To Face With Society's Lepers

Downtown Night Ministry

By Dean C. Jones, Ph.D.

Fairway Press
Lima, Ohio

FACE TO FACE WITH SOCIETY'S LEPERS:
DOWNTOWN NIGHT MINISTRY

BV
4456
.J66
1991

FIRST EDITION
Copyright © 1991 by
Dean C. Jones

7755 / ISBN 1-55673-299-6   PRINTED IN U.S.A.

To Norm and Bonnie Riggins for 22 years of ministry to Seattle's downtown night community.

Acknowledgements

Many people have helped in the process of this project. My wife, Stella, has shared in the ten years of ministry represented by this book. She also served as one of the reviewers of the manuscript. Larry Baker, Ray Heckendorn and Herb Adams also made important comments on the work in process. A much earlier draft of similar material was reviewed by Mel Foreman. The title of this edition was suggested by Ray Heckendorn. Computer assistance was given by Alta Long and Robert McGeeney. Many professionals contributed by sharing published and unpublished material. These people are listed in the text and in a final notation on references.

Unfortunately the real heroes of this book can not be acknowledged by name. When their stories appear names have been changed to protect anonymity. But a very special word of thanks must be given.

I am also deeply indebted to the ministry of Operation Nightwatch for giving me the opportunity to serve. My first introduction to the program came in a meeting with Bud Palmberg. Since then I have had the total encouragement of Norm Riggins. In the cities where I have worked many volunteers have been a source of personal inspiration. Board members have also given in a variety of ways to me personally and to the work of ministry. George T. Guernsey III in St, Louis stands out as a good example of dedication at the level of Board membership. At the time of his death he was the Chairperson of the Board of Directors for the St. Louis program. As a retired banker he gave unselfishly to assist a number of service programs. More recently I have been blessed by the efforts of the Board for Tacoma's program. The Seattle Operation Nightwatch Board of Directors took the critical step in standing behind this book project.

The staff of C.S.S. Publishing Company has been most helpful in bringing this effort to a final stage. Ellen Shockey was enthusiastic about the project. Fred Steiner showed considerable patience in working through many editorial changes.

A final word of thanks to you for walking the street with me in the pages that follow. I pray that you will find some point of blessing in the experiences and information I share.

Table of Contents

Introduction

This book is planned as a journey with the reader into problems everyone has some familiarity with. Many have personal and professional experience far beyond mine in any given area I discuss. Hopefully, however, the material will provide some new insights on how to respond to downtown problems from a Christian perspective.

The pages contain many references to actual events and people on the streets of different cities. These scenarios, with a few exceptions, come from personal experience doing the work of ministry in a program called Operation Nightwatch. The shared late-night encounters occurred on the streets of Seattle, Washington; Portland, Oregon; St. Louis, Missouri; Denver, Colorado; Hollywood, California; and Tacoma, Washington.

I first learned of late-night, downtown ministry when introduced to the Rev. Bud Palmberg, founder of Seattle's Operation Nightwatch, in 1969. In 1979 the Rev. Norm Riggins, Director of the Seattle program, gave me an opportunity to serve as a volunteer. This became a full-time commitment in 1983.

The following chapters take the reader into places ranging from Skid Road taverns to fancy cocktail lounges, bus depots to hospital emergency rooms and downtown streets. Most of the interaction reported took place between the hours of 10:00 p.m. and 2:00 a.m. The people who are introduced may sound familiar. Folks like them can be found in all major cities.

Any form of "street ministry" is assumed to focus primarily on "street people." The pages of this book reveal a wide range of people on the city streets late at night. The homeless and economically displaced are given center stage in chapter two. The term "Skid Road" may be confusing to the reader. It is now more popular to use the term "Skid Row." The image of a road is more in keeping with the original use of the term. It was coined in Seattle, Washington, as a way to identify that part of downtown growing up around the place where logs were skidded down to waterfront saw mills over a surface of greased logs tied together. Early taverns and flop houses flourished as part of this male dominated domain. City mission activity concentrated on this segment of downtown. During the past two decades most cities have undergone dramatic changes. Skid Road areas can still be found, sometimes occupying huge portions of downtown as in Los Angeles. But new office buildings and shops are fast replacing old taverns and flop houses. Downtown land values have risen sharply. Tall buildings reach for the sky. Closed doors, concrete/glass walls and faceless strangers now shape the sidewalk environment and pose new challenges to downtown ministry.

The homeless of yesterday could find sources of help in the informal network of Skid Road. At one time downtown taverns formed a loose network of social service, giving such information as where to find work and where to stay for the night. Today those who are homeless in the city are more likely to face social isolation and stigmatization. This is reinforced by the hysteria around drugs and violence. These changes make downtown ministry both more important and considerably more challenging. Adding to the difficulty is the pull of the more affluent part of today's downtown. Is it good stewardship of a minister's time to enter the fancy cocktail lounges when the down and out cry for help? This book will not give ultimate answers to these challenges. It should, however, contribute to our general understanding of the city as a mission field and selected problems wherever they are found.

The first section of the book is primarily a sharing of encounters in Operation Nightwatch arranged under the general topics of homelessness, alcoholism, drug addiction, suicide and mental illness. These chapters, beginning with chapter 2, follow a similar format. First background information is given, then personal glimpses drawn from work on the street at night and finally a discussion of responses to problems. Chapter 7 is a discussion of selected issues important in the process of preaching the Gospel in the City. Some of these issues are very practical since they grow out of experience in ministry on the street. For example, there is a consideration of the city sidewalk as social space and the social setting of a tavern. The chapter and the first section of the book end with a few words about burn out in ministry.

In the second section of the book additional information is given on alcoholism, drug addiction, suicide and mental illness. This portion of the book will not be of interest to all readers. It suggests the kind of material becoming more important for those of us in ministry who want to keep in touch with work in other disciplines. One of the major challenges today is to relate to people from a holistic reference. This will call for an increasing awareness of many different contributions to the helping process. Christian ministry, however, will never become a simple compilation of the best from social work, psychology and sociology. The Great Commission remains to go and make disciples. This will always be the major theme for those who champion the Kingdom of God.

Chapter 1
Meet The Lepers

"Why don't you tell your volunteers to work the night places that are out of the immediate downtown area?" This advice came from a police captain in a West Coast city where the downtown night scene was dominated by considerable drug dealing. As mentioned in the introduction, the downtown area of most cities includes considerable variety in the types of places open at night. Although well-defined Skid Road areas are not as obvious as in the past, most cities have areas known for high crime rates. Professionals, including ministers, are not expected to be in these parts of town during the day and especially not at night. The police officer made it clear to me that he considered the Cubans, Mexicans and other "losers" as beyond any form of outreach. They were seen as "lepers." Street ministry touches the lepers of society.

In most cases the concept of being untouchable refers to specific types of people. Other times it refers to a state of being or an experience that is more psychological than physically untouchable. In either case street ministry, especially late-night ministry, must move in to walk where others choose not to tread. I am thinking, for example, of a late-night call from the emergency room of a city hospital. A middle-aged wife and mother had died only minutes before after an auto accident. It was my duty as a minister to remain with the immediate family for some three hours of intense grief. In a similar situation the death came shortly before I entered the emergency room area on my regular rounds. I went into the special room reserved for family members and again sat and cried with close family members. Another type of situation that also elicits a "hands off" attitude is the disease of AIDS. The list of untouchables would also include those cases where advanced cancer is present. For many the word "suicide" also conjures up an immediate feeling of wanting to withdraw from

11

the interaction. Leper type situations, including untouchable or unmentionable feelings, behaviors or conditions, call for the highest level of Christian commitment on the part of those who become involved.

In this chapter many different people are introduced as examples of ministry that dares to reach out in face-to-face contact with society's lepers. These people were seen in cities where the author worked in late-night out reach.

"Father, It's So Good To See You"

This greeting came from a thin, blond woman in her early 20s. Mary was a regular on the downtown streets of Tacoma, Washington. She always had a ready smile for me. But she often squirmed and twisted her fingers as she avoided my eyes when talking about doing drugs. The first night I saw her she was standing on a street corner, waiting for her next trick. Several weeks went by before I saw her again. This time she seemed different. She talked about taking classes to become a beautician. She said that she wanted to get off the streets.

The fluctuations in appearance and mood that I saw in Mary are typical of most cases of drug addiction. Talk of getting off the street and looking fairly normal contrast with withdrawal and haggard looks on other occasions. In the case of Mary she was generally with others, making it hard to engage her in serious conversation. One night when she stood alone on the sidewalk she held out her arm for me to see. There was noticeable inflammation along her needle tracks. She talked of being in the hospital. The arm was swollen up "like a football." The infection episode from excessive injections of drugs scared her. She felt that she should do something. Her reaction was to reduce her intake of drugs. She told me that she was doing "only" two shots of heroin a day. Based on her normal pattern she felt that this was a sign of progress. But she was still living with a fellow who was actively dealing in drugs.

A few weeks after the above contact, Mary came running up to me on the street. She said that she had been looking all over for me. That day she had been released from jail after serving a two-week sentence. She was proud of the fact that she had been off drugs for that amount of time. She said that she came down to the street that night just to prove to herself, to her friends, and to me that she could say no. So far she had been able to refuse all offers of drugs. While in jail she attended a church service. She was surprised to learn that God would forgive her. As she saw it, she had done far too many "bad things." The image of this young woman with a sparkle in her eyes and an eagerness to reach out to people haunts me as I realize how deeply she was involved in the drug culture of the city streets at that time. I have not seen Mary recently and have no idea where she might be at the present time.

Alone Without Hope

He wore a plaid jacket. This man with a full, white beard was in his mid 60s. I greeted him late one night as he stepped out of a Skid Road tavern near 21st and Larimer in Denver, Colorado. When Stan noticed my clergy collar he immediately pulled a small New Testament out of an inside jacket pocket. Next he reached into another pocket and pulled out a large leather sheath holding a sharp knife. After displaying and then carefully replacing these objects Stan walked with me along a dark sidewalk leading away from the tavern.

As we walked and talked Stan first tried to impress me with a strong macho image. He said that he had made $25 that day while panhandling uptown. He talked about doing 10 years in prison. This hard time was for murder. As he explained it, he actually killed three men, two while in the service and one on the street.

Before too long the strong image this stranger tried to convey began to fade. He seemed to need to share some very deep feelings about a brother. This brother was a strong hero,

13

giving years of his life in service to God as the director of a mission in Portland, Oregon. But unfortunately this man of God developed a severe case of diabetes and then underwent surgery during which both legs were amputated. This became an obsession with Stan. He just could not see how a God of Love would do such a thing to his brother.

The sharing about his brother brought tears to Stan's eyes. He admitted frequent episodes of crying himself to sleep beside the railroad tracks in strange cities. When sleep came he was often tormented by nightmares. Visions of a final judgment scene dominated these nightmares. He saw himself standing before a large book. An angel looked carefully for his name in the book but never found it. Stan hated God but could not stand the thought of an eternity without God. That night on a downtown street corner I shared with him in ministry and ended the exchange by placing a hand on his shoulder and praying as cars passed on the street near by.

I Am a Run-Away

It was after midnight. I was tired and feeling like I should call it a night. But I decided to make one more round of the downtown streets in Tacoma. As I passed a bus stop area I noticed two fellows sitting back from the sidewalk. One of the two noticed me and called out as I approached. As I moved closer to the two strangers they appeared as a study in contrasts. One was an elderly man who was wearing a heavy jacket. He was lost in a rhythmic action, moving his arms constantly and staring vacantly into space. It was not possible to include him in a conversation. The other fellow was a young boy. This boy, Jim, said that he was 15 years old. His brown hair fell down over his eyes and covered his ears. He wore tennis shoes with no shoestrings.

Jim wanted me to know that he was a runaway from a group home in the city. He had been on the run for several days, going to Seattle where he ate and slept in a mission. As he saw his situation one of the other boys in the group home was "out to get him." Fear of this other boy was the motivation for running away. But now he wanted to return. It was getting cold. He did not have a coat. He was hungry. He did not have any money.

I called the runaway hot line and the police and waited with him for an officer to arrive. What does a 15-year-old runaway think about on the downtown streets? Jim wanted to talk about the church services he could remember. Obviously, the presence of a "man of the cloth" served as a reinforcement for such talk. But I wonder if the thoughts would not be present even if they were not so reinforced. As he kicked at the concrete curb with a well-worn tennis shoe, Jim broke into the spontaneous singing of stanzas from gospel songs.

Another significant area of interest for this kid of the streets was memory about his parents. He talked for some time about his father. I was informed that the father played a musical instrument in a local band and lived "not far from here." There was never a negative word about the father. Jim also spoke about a stepmother. Again, there were no words of condemnation. At the time I wondered if these parents knew that their teenager was a runaway and that he really cared about them. When the police officer came and Jim left I became keenly aware of how blessed I was in having family to share with.

Meeting Under an Umbrella

One rainy, dark night I walked the downtown streets of Portland, Oregon carrying a black umbrella. Tom, a man in his early 20s came up to me to beg for a cigarette. When he saw my clergy collar he changed his request into a plea for a listening ear. Together we walked under the protective covering of a building entrance that offered some relief from the torrents of rain.

Tom first wanted me to know that he was out of the hospital "against medical advice." He pulled a loose-fitting shirt back away from his right shoulder to display deep scars. I was told that he had undergone many surgical procedures for bone cancer. They wanted him to stay in the hospital. But he walked away. Cancer was only one of many heavy concerns hounding Tom. One of his most painful memories involved the loss of his wife and a small child. There was an automobile accident. Tom was driving the car. Both his wife and child were killed. He could not understand why he wasn't taken with them. He repeatedly said that he should have died or that he was going to die.

After sharing his trauma around the death of family members, I was then invited to journey back in time with Tom to Vietnam. He talked at length about the times of killing while in the service. For him the killing had become a personal affair for which he felt guilt. To add to his problems Tom was an alcoholic. He had gone through treatment and was on Antabuse. That night he said that he was on "downers." He freely admitted that he was on the way to make a delivery of drugs. He showed no real interest in living. He talked about death as the most likely possibility for him in the very near future.

When it became my turn to respond to his litany of pain and guilt, I said something like, "I assume that you want some response from me as a minister. Are you wanting me to pray with you?" When Tom replied in the affirmative, I invited him to gather up all of his agony and then to hold it up to God. Then I placed a hand on his shoulder and began to pray. But after only a few words Tom stopped me. He said, "There's something else, I've killed a man." I instructed him to add this to the list of things and to hold it all up to God. As we prayed, Tom reached out once to gently hold me back away from the rain that was falling just beyond the reach of the umbrella. As we parted he reached into his pocket to give me all of his money. I refused the money, informing him that my reward was in serving as a minister to folks on the street at night.

16

"I Don't Know How to Do A Funeral"

Ray called me aside on a downtown sidewalk in Tacoma late one night. I could not remember meeting him before, but he seemed to know who I was. When we were out of sight from others on the sidewalk, I noticed tears in his eyes. He was holding a tin can with coins in it. Ray's first words to me were "I don't know how to do a funeral, could you help?" Then he told me that his young wife had died. He was taking up a collection to buy her a fit dress to be buried in. He wanted her to be cremated. The ashes were to be thrown overboard out in the bay. Ray asked if I would go along in the boat, say something appropriate and release the ashes. I hesitated for a minute, wondering if this was a set-up to get rid of me. But Ray's sincerity seemed real and so I agreed.

I should not have been so hesitant. As it turned out, Ray was never able to follow through on any of the funeral details. I set up a time to view the body with him. He did not show up. I learned later that he was in the hospital under treatment for both a heart problem and withdrawal from heroin. When he was released from the hospital I talked with him about new plans for a funeral. But when a specific time was set Ray was again not available. This second time he was in jail.

The young woman was buried. Only her parents and a few close family members were present. Ray was mad at the family for making decisions without him. They in turn, were very bitter toward him and his lifestyle which they felt had something to do with the woman's death. I listened to one very angry telephone conversation between Ray and the mother of the deceased. In the course of the conversation Ray informed her that he had always felt that she was against him in the inter-racial marriage. He went on to tell her that he made more money in one week than she made in a year. I assume that Ray was selling drugs and also working as a pimp. I have not seen him in over a year.

Old and Alone

As I walked through the Trailways depot in St. Louis around midnight I saw Jane sitting at a table in the restaurant area. A big smile revealed two gold teeth, in strong contrast to the brown of her face. Jane always had at least two large plastic bags full of all kinds of odds and ends. She sat alone drinking coffee. I approached her and started a conversation. The possibility of contact with people was the main downtown attraction for this senior citizen. She admitted to being "at least" 80 years old. I always warned her about the dangers of being downtown at night. But I never convinced her that she should remain inside her apartment just out of the immediate downtown area.

One night I gave this elderly widow a ride home. That was the beginning of a relationship lasting until I left St. Louis. I joked with Jane as I carried her bags to the car. We developed a little ritual. First I warned her about being downtown and then I offered to give her a ride home. She seemed to wait all day for this ride. It was important that I be the one to take her home. I told her that she could not always count on me. But this did not keep her from making repeated trips downtown, hoping to see me. She talked about many things from her past as we drove together through the deserted downtown streets late at night. I learned that she had worked in a local factory during World War II, something she seemed very proud of. She also spoke of a husband who walked off and left her. She said that she had outlived all of her family. I never understood what she meant by references to keeping a house where there was dancing and drinking on the premises. This elderly woman and I were more like family than two strangers as we drove from downtown St. Louis out to her subsidized housing unit near Forest Park. It was very hard for me to say goodbye to this friend when I left St. Louis to return to the West Coast.

Black Tights and Leather Belt

My work in Denver was in those parts of the city where no tourist went. Late at night I often entered a neighborhood near East Colfax downtown that had a reputation for violence. The parking lot of a 7-11 store in this area became a staging ground for a shoot out one night. One tavern in the neighborhood was a frequent stop for me. The regular patrons occasionally directed solicitous comments on personal safety toward me. One stranger proceeded to lecture me on how to protect myself. He accentuated his remarks with demonstrations on such fine details as how to use a coat in self-defense against an attacker with a knife. Although he knew the language of self-defense he apparently was not able to follow his own advice. He admitted that he had been brutally beaten on many occasions. His jaw had been broken, teeth knocked out and ribs dislocated. He was looking for trouble and often found it. I went into the same places where he went and I was never attacked. In this tavern and in that neighborhood, violence was a way of life. Those at highest risk were the people living in the area.

Two people in particular stand out in my memory of that tavern off East Colfax in Denver. One was a middle-aged man and the other a woman who talked about black tights and a leather belt. The man, Steve, was an alcoholic. He lived in a cheap apartment above the tavern. One night this stranger invited me up to his apartment so that we could talk more freely. He also wanted to give me a soft drink as an indication of his friendliness. While visiting him, he insisted on taking me down a dark, dirty hall to meet one of his friends. This friend, an elderly man, was a prisoner in his small rented room. He was a late-stage alcoholic. When I saw him he was wearing a ragged undershirt as he sat beside a wooden table drinking wine from a paper cup. He seldom went out of the room.

During my encounters in the tavern and the visit in his room, I talked with Steve about many things. He was interested in religion, but had no strong church connections. Steve made a great deal about the fact that he always helped others. He was a major "care giver" for his apartment building. One of his major tasks was to ensure the regular flow of cheap wine from a near-by store to his fellow alcoholics. He was very busy on the day when the Social Security and SSI checks arrived in the mail. My most impressive meeting with Steve was the time I saw him in the county jail. He was being held on a charge of stealing a pack of cigarettes from one of the largest chain grocery stores in the city. By the time I found out where he was and made my visit he had been in jail for some 30 days. He could never raise the $10 bail money. He was very surprised to see me. I called the Public Defender's office after my visit and Steve was released the following day.

The woman I remember from the Denver tavern was a middle-aged woman who first noticed my I.D. badge as I sat at the bar drinking a Coke. Sarah said that she knew Operation Nightwatch in Seattle. She spoke at length about her many talks with Rev. Norman Riggins, Director of Seattle's Operation Nightwatch. When I first met her she seemed overwhelmed by all of the problems she had encountered since moving to Denver from Seattle. We walked together away from the bar to a booth near the tavern's juke box. The loud sound of a familiar country western song provided background music for our conversation.

Sarah first explained to me that she had major financial problems in Denver immediately after her arrival. When she could not get any form of assistance she turned to stealing from local food stores. One of her regular practices was to hide steaks under her coat and then walk out of a store. She was picked up by the police on one occasion and taken to jail. I was given the details of what she considered to be an invasion of privacy during the process of the body search as part of the detention process. After her release from jail, Sarah got a job at a junk yard. When she found out that the owner could not read she proceeded to steal from him by telling him check amounts that were not accurate.

The black tights and leather belt came into the conversation as Sarah explained how she sold her body to get money. I think that she was building a good case for the fact that she was beyond the reach of God's love, something I have heard from many others. During the time when she was desperate for money a man offered her $75. He first asked her to put on a pair of black tights. When she was dressed in this outfit he removed his clothes. Then he handed her his heavy leather belt and urged her to hit him with it. She complied and earned her $75. But she was not proud of her role in this scene.

As we talked in the tavern, Sarah spoke very sincerely about a desire for forgiveness. She said that she carried a bottle of water from Seattle, calling it her "holy water." But she got little consolation from this bottle. We talked of God's redemptive love, a topic she was not unfamiliar with given her previous contacts with Rev. Riggins. With a country western tune playing on the juke box I invited this woman to look to God in prayer. I prayed and then instructed her to lift her concerns and guilt to God in prayer. At least for a brief moment, that tavern in one of the roughest parts of downtown Denver became a sacred place.

A 92-Year-Old Shopping Bag Lady

Strands of gray hair, a weathered face and frail body were the most obvious features of Martha, a 92-year-old who had lived on the downtown streets of St. Louis for eight years. I first met her in the Greyhound depot late at night. She was carrying two plastic bags. During one of my early contacts, Martha sat in the fast food section of the depot, drinking coffee she had purchased on the premises and eating chocolate covered raisins she was carrying in one of her bags. When I sat down with her in the booth she offered me some of the raisins and seemed glad to talk with me.

During the first several months of contact with Martha she shared many of her impressions of the turn of events resulting in her habitat on the streets of the city. Her husband died years ago. Before his death he talked about taking her on a trip. They never took the trip. Now she spends long hours every day and night in the downtown bus depots. Martha also told me about the sale of her house and how her children "stole" money from her. When she gave me the address of this residence I drove out to the suburbs to check the situation out. I was hoping that I could get some lead on the whereabouts of her children. The address she gave me turned out to be a place of business. I was able to talk to a nearby neighbor. This man was familiar with Martha and the family. He said that the children had tried to get Martha off the streets but that she would not cooperate.

On the street, I watched as things went from bad to worse for this 92-year-old grandmother. I was never successful in contacting her children. At times Martha would talk to me and other times she turned away from me, refusing all attempts on my part to communicate. One night she asked me if I was married. When I said yes, she wanted to know why I was not at home with my wife. She then said that I was a poor husband and turned her back to me. A few nights later she seemed especially distressed. This time she did talk. She said that someone had taken her purse and all of her money. I gave her a few dollars to carry her through the night until she could contact another resource in the morning.

One particularly hard episode for me was the time Martha was committed to the city's mental hospital. When I learned from contacts on the street that she had been committed, I made my way to the hospital to pay her a visit. She obviously recognized me, but would not talk. She sat in the main lobby area of her ward, tearing Kleenex tissues into small pieces and stuffing those into her purse. After her two weeks in the mental hospital she seemed to be worse than before. She went from carrying two plastic bags to six or eight large plastic bags and was very withdrawn.

My last contact with Martha came on a cold St. Louis night during the winter. I was approaching the bus depot around midnight when I ran into her as she was coming out of the depot. She mumbled something about being forced to leave because she did not have a bus ticket. As she stood with her hands in tight fists against her light coat I told her that I would find a place for her to sleep. I became directive with her, instructing her to take my hand. I held onto her as we walked slowly across a downtown intersection. As we crossed with the light, I noticed that she was having real difficulty determining the pattern of light changes in the darkness. I thought of the potential danger for her with this vision limitation as she walked from bus depot to bus depot in the darknes. That night my car was not far away. I helped her into the front seat. After a short drive to one of the emergency shelters in St. Louis I helped her up a short flight of stairs. As we waited together for the door to open, Martha turned to me and said "thanks." Sometimes when the weather turns cold and I am out on a downtown street I think of Martha and hope that she did get home to her daughters. I do not know the end of the story in her case or in many other cases where I touch for only a brief period of time.

My Pastor Is An Alcoholic

Bill sat at the bar in St. Louis's Sheraton Hotel. I often began the night's shift in this place, talking with the bartender and waiting for volunteers. This spotless bar managed by a formally attired bartender was hard for me to get used to after the round of Skid Road bars I had seen in other cities. On my first visit to the Sheraton Hotel Cocktail Lounge I stared in amazement at the sight of a fancy dishwasher in motion. As the glasses from the bar were washed to a spotless sparkle I could not help thinking of a bar in Portland, Oregon where cockroaches danced in the semi-darkness. In that bar the bartender once informed me that a customer had been stabbed in the back while sitting where I was sitting and that this man was now a quadriplegic. The Sheraton Lounge was indeed a different kind of night place for me!

I met Bill in the lounge. He was a business man. He was wearing a three piece suit. He had been at the bar for some time, but was not drunk. He was staying in the hotel while looking for work. When I seemed interested in listening he talked on and on about his personal situation. For starters he informed me that he was separated from his wife. A divorce was pending. As he saw the situation, his work stress and other sources of stress had been too much for the marriage. One of the major areas of stress, as he saw it, was his own involvement in the lives of other people. He told me that he had spent too much time trying to help his pastor who was an alcoholic. The pastor did get help for the alcoholism with Bill's assistance, but Bill was left with a shattered marriage. Now he was trying to put his life back together again. On that particular night volunteers would be meeting me before going out on the street. This group included a Catholic priest, a Presbyterian pastor and a Lutheran pastor. I invited Bill to join the group for prayer in a corner of the cocktail lounge. He was glad for the opportunity. After the prayers one of the volunteers stayed with him for three hours to help him sort out his situation.

A Young Man Out of Work and Depressed

In Denver I made a late-night telephone number accessible to people in need. One night after going to bed, I got a call from a man who said that he was calling from an all-night restaurant. He spoke of serious problems and talked about hurting himself. I told him that I would meet him in the restaurant. I dressed and drove a short distance for this after hours meeting.

John was a young man in his late 20s. His facial expression, general body language and verbal expressions all pointed to a very depressed state. I ordered hot tea for both of us. As we sat in a booth that night John told me that he could not find work and that he had thought of "ending it all." I talked openly with him about suicide. My part of the exchange included words of hope and encouragement as well as some practical suggestions. I told him to explore the want ads and other resources for a job. I made a contract with him not to take his life before our next meeting two days later.

During the second meeting John shared his experiences in looking for work. We talked again about suicide. I had learned on the first meeting the method he had thought of using. He talked about taking some pills. I checked on the lethality of these pills. On this second meeting I informed John that I wanted him to throw the pills away. Then I gave him specific instructions. I told him to get in his car and that I would follow him in my car to his apartment so that I could watch him destroy the potentially lethal pills. He agreed to this. I followed him home where we surprised his wife by our entrance. John went into a bedroom and came back with a bottle of pills. I watched as he threw them into the sink and turned on the garbage disposal.

John had contacts with a few churches in Denver. Part of our exchange included his personal quest for a life of faith. But most of the attention turned to the immediate problems of getting a job and coping with options other than suicide as a way to respond to a crisis. John did get a job. He called me one night, very excited. When I met him at the restaurant he was wearing a new Texaco uniform. This time he paid for the hot tea. A few days later John and his wife invited me for a lunch of bologna sandwiches and tomato soup to celebrate the new turn of events in their young married life. I wish that I could say that this story ended with instantaneous success but it did not. A few weeks later John was fired from his job. He was again back in the struggle of how to handle his situation. I am not sure how much long-term good came out of the short period of contact I had with him.

Get Me A Club, I'm Going to Kill Someone

Words pleading for a murder weapon were the last words to come from the lips of a big man who was well known and well liked on Portland's streets. Jake wanted only to help people. He was never the one to start trouble. I did not know him personally. He came to my attention only at the time of his death.

On the night of Jake's death, I began the evening shift as usual at about 10:00 p.m. near Burnside Street in downtown Portland, Oregon. That night I was giving a new recruit to the program of Operation Nightwatch his first solo experience on the street. We agreed to go separate routes and to meet back in front of one of the popular Skid Road taverns around midnight. As I walked back to that tavern shortly before midnight, I saw an emergency vehicle and a small crowd gathered just outside a roped off area immediately in front of the tavern. Closer to the scene, bright lights were focused on a silent body stretched out on the sidewalk. Paramedics were pounding the huge chest of a man. The man's shirt had been ripped off.

A thin plastic tube ran from a bottle held high over the body of this man into his left arm where a bandage covered the point of entry into his chest. I recognized the young man who stood with blood spotted T-shirt holding the intravenous arrangement. He was new to the street, recently out of the state prison on parole after serving time for a major crime. He was also one of the most racist of the people on the street. This night he was just trying to help as he held the life-support bottle above the fallen friend. But his efforts and the work of the paramedics and others was of little consequence. Jake was rolled over and onto a stretcher. The ambulance drove slowly away from the scene. There was no need to hurry. Jake was dead.

I was told about the events preceding the arrival of the medical crisis team. Jake saw two men fighting in front of the tavern. He tried to separate them. Someone driving by misinterpreted what was going on, thinking that Jake was attacking one of the men. The man in the passing car jumped out of the car, knife in hand. Before Jake had a chance to defend himself this stranger plunged the knife into his chest, cutting major blood vessels near the heart. Jake reeled toward the door of the tavern, yelled for a club to kill his assailant, then fell to the sidewalk, dead. One of my responsibilities was to comfort the bereaved. Jake was well liked and sorely missed by many. I was also concerned about the new recruit for the program. I wondered if this scene would give him second thoughts about wanting to become a late night minister. But he did continue as a volunteer in the Portland program.

An 8-Year-Old Street Person

One night in St. Louis when I was with one of the volunteers, we watched as a young boy, blue eyes and dirty face, played the video machines in a downtown bus depot. At first we thought that Tony was with some older boys. But when the older fellows left he stayed, begging money so that he could play the machines again. We were distracted by other situations and when we looked for him again he had disappeared.

Since we knew where other video machines were located in the downtown area, we started looking for Tony. It did not take long to find him again. This time we took him aside and spent some time listening to his story. He had not yet been home from school. He was eight years old. He was afraid that his father would beat him up again. He did not know what to do. He did warm up to the idea of a McDonald's kid's meal. We purchased the food for him and called both the police and child protective services. We sat with Tony until the police came. In subsequent communication with the child protective services we learned that Tony and his family were well known to the agency. There had been many reports of neglect of the children. The father was an alcoholic. I am not sure how the situation was resolved by the agency. As I recall, there were six or eight children in the family.

To Cut Christmas Trees

When I started working as a volunteer in Seattle's Operation Nightwatch I was very curious about the different people on the night scene. I was especially interested in the men who rode the freight trains into and out of town. One night I met two of these modern transients and immediately wanted to learn from them what it was like to ride through the night in an open railroad box car. The details of that night's encounter which follow below do give a little insight into this life style. But the narrative is most important as another look at the kinds of situations and people encountered in late-night ministry.

On the night when I met these two modern nomads it was raining heavily. The weather is one very important factor in the life of a street minister. In more traditional, office bound ministry the weather is not as important. That night I carried a black umbrella as I ducked into a downtown tavern that is one of the oldest gay bars in the country. After folding the umbrella and shaking out the excess water I sat at the bar with a glass of Coke. In a few minutes two men came through the front door of the place, followed by a burst of cold wind. Both men carried large back packs. One man was average in height. His buddy was tall and thin. This second man used the street name "Too Tall." From their appearance and mannerisms I assumed that these men were strangers in town and that they had no idea they were in a gay bar. They found places to sit, dropped their back packs to the floor and ordered a pitcher of beer.

As it turned out the shorter of the two strangers, Bob, sat down next to me. When he noticed that I was a minister he was friendly, offering to buy me a Coke. We talked. Over the course of a few minutes I learned that the two had arrived in

Seattle by freight train from the midwest. They had heard about temporary work near Portland cutting Christmas trees. The switching yard for trains going to Portland was some 20 miles south of Seattle near Auburn. They had considered hitchhiking but the heavy rain made this a very difficult chore. I listened to both men for some time before deciding that I would offer them a ride.

When I mentioned a free ride to Auburn, these two strangers left a half-empty pitcher of beer on the bar, gathered up their back-packs and followed me out of the tavern. Outside I held my umbrella overhead as we loaded the back-packs into the trunk of my car. Then the shorter man slid into the middle of the front seat while Too Tall sat next to the door on the passenger's side. I drove south out of Seattle, the windshield wipers trying to keep up with the torrents of rain.

Bob talked for the first few miles before the warmth and steady motion of the car lulled him to sleep. His talk was all about the experience of spending time in "every detox and jail on the West Coast." Too Tall asked if he could "play the radio." He then proceeded to switch from station to station over the range of the dial until he found a country western station. We drove through the darkness with the music playing at high volume. At one point, I was not sure which road to take. I asked Too Tall if he knew where to go. He said that he had never been south of Seattle by car.

Somewhere along the way Too Tall said that he really wanted to see a dog a friend was keeping for him. I followed his directions as we turned off the Interstate to drive down lonely, dirt roads. We found a house that Too Tall recognized but there was no dog. He did not want to disturb the people in the house. When we were far from other cars on seldom traveled back roads Too Tall informed me that he was on probation for murder. I did not see this as the best place or time for such an announcement! As he explained the situation a man in the freight yard in Spokane, Washington tried to steal something from his bags. Knives were pulled and Too Tall cut the man who later died in the Emergency Room of a local hospital. The court action accused Too Tall but also recognized a measure of self-defense. I was certainly not made comfortable with the knowledge that I was driving down back roads in the dark with someone holding a conviction for murder.

We did get back to the Interstate. I was able to find the location in Auburn where these men wanted to go. They were both very thankful for the ride. Too Tall gave me a Seattle bus transfer and a pair of sun glasses he found on the street as "payment" for the help. I did not learn much about what it is like to ride the rails. I did have the experience of sharing a few hours with two men who were very thankful for a helping hand in the middle of the night.

"You Gotta Meet My Wife"

One night on a downtown Denver side street I found Jack, a 55-year-old man, standing outside a tavern. As I passed him I said "how're you doing." Jack was eager to talk about his situation. In language that staggered with the insult of a recent indulgence in cheap wine Jack informed me that he had been 86'd from the tavern. They would not let him in because he had a reputation for creating a disturbance. He informed me that he was "good man." After we chatted for a few minutes on the sidewalk Jack said that he wanted to take me home so that I could meet his wife.

The two of us crossed a downtown street in the middle of the block. I followed Jack as he made his way down an alley toward a large apartment building. On the back porch of this building he stopped in front of a door to something resembling a broom closet. He opened the small door. As I stood looking over his shoulder I could see the tattered clothes, long beard and glassy eyes of a middle-aged man collapsed into a fetal position within the narrow confines of the box-like closet. Jack mumbled a greeting, took a new bottle of wine out of a coat pocket and handed it over to the gaunt figure in the box on the porch. This man carefully closed his fingers around the bottle. He never uttered a word. Jack closed the small door with a comment about "keeping a friend alive."

Once inside the apartment building, I followed Jack up a flight of stairs and down a carpeted hall. He stopped in front of one door and knocked. A woman's voice came through the door. Jack said that he had a friend. The woman said that she did not want to meet any of his friends. He persisted and she finally opened the door. When this woman saw my clergy collar she apologized to me, saying that Jack often brought his drinking buddies home. The apartment was pleasantly furnished and comfortably warm.

After introductions, Jack began a long tirade against the woman who sat beside him in her cotton housecoat. He said that his wife would not help him. He blamed her for all of his problems. He just didn't know what to do about her. At some point in the talking he asked me to "pray for them." I first spoke directly to his wife and then prayed.

When Jack ran out of energy for verbal abuse his wife spoke in a level, controlled voice. She said that I should hear her side of the story. That very week she had returned home after a period of hospitalization. The trip to the hospital in an emergency vehicle followed a severe beating that necessitated a number of stitches to close an open cut from an attack by her husband during one of his drunken binges. In sharp contrast to his accusations against her, she informed me that she was the one who worked cleaning houses to pay the rent and keep them in food. He was not able to hold down a job with his full-time commitment to alcohol. She said that she was a recovering alcoholic. She was fearful of how much longer she could keep going to AA with the kind of abuse she suffered at his hands. His regular physical beating of her seemed to be his major contribution to the marriage. Jack did not have a ready response to the reality confrontation.

After leaving the apartment that night I determined to make another visit without the husband. A few days later during an afternoon I did return. The woman was home alone. She was glad to see me. Her first comment was that she felt that I had "really blessed" the home when I prayed during the late night visit. We talked about her options. She felt that she could get a better job, but was hesitant about how to handle her alcoholic husband. I gave strong support for her to leave him if necessary to protect herself. She had considered separation but needed reinforcement for taking such a move in the expression of "tough love." I told her that she was important and that I did not want to see her destroyed by the increasingly severe beatings her husband gave.

Fear of Cancer

In Denver, I could recognize many of the regulars on the street near 21st and Larimer. This was a major Skid Road turf. When people who obviously were not part of this scene suddenly appeared they were not difficult to spot. One night a well dressed young man was walking along Larimer Street alone. He had been doing some drinking but was not drunk. His presence in that part of town was a curiosity for me so I made it a point to approach him to introduce myself.

After only a few words of greeting Ken told his story. He said that he had made the trip to Denver by bus to enter the VA facility for drug rehabilitation. This was the message he left with his stepmother in Wyoming. But he did not tell her the whole story. Before leaving his home town in Wyoming he was given a complete medical exam. After this exam he was told that he had cancer. Now he was walking the streets of Skid Road, running from his physical condition. He had not told anyone about the cancer.

I asked Ken if I could call his stepmother. He gave me her telephone number, telling me to call collect. I had no intention of telling her about the cancer, feeling that this was his privilege. I did want to get some verification of the pending VA treatment. When I talked with the stepmother she

32

supported Ken's story about his acceptance for treatment at the local VA hospital. I next talked to Ken and worked with him about the need to follow through with hospitalization. After some talking he agreed to go with me to the hospital. I drove him across town, away from the 21st and Larimer scene to the VA hospital.

Trying to Get Into a State Mental Hospital

It was after 1:00 a.m. when I got a call from a hospital in Tacoma. The Emergency Room personnel were concerned about a 27-year-old woman. This woman was not going to be admitted. She had no place to go. She had hitchhiked from Seattle heading for the state mental hospital near Tacoma. Jill had both a physical impairment and a history of mental illness. Two days before she had attempted suicide. Most of the time she was able to work and to take care of herself in her own apartment while taking regular medication. But I saw her during a time of acute stress. She said that she felt like "everything was falling apart" and that "no one was interested" in her.

There are specific steps to take in such a situation in Washington State and other states. Normally, a mental health professional becomes involved. If a commitment procedure must be initiated this professional initiates the process. A patient does not admit himself/herself into a state hospital. Jill wanted to be admitted. But she walked away from a general hospital before she could be seen by a mental health professional. I talked with some of the key people in emergency services and learned that Jill was considered a "difficult case" in Seattle, her place of residence. She was inclined to abuse the system, making it hard for professionals to take her seriously when she did get into a crisis situation. She had been into a number of different clinics during the day before I saw her late that night. In one of these clinics, she was restrained with leg holds while waiting for an examination.

I did not feel that it would be appropriate to dump this woman on the street. In this and in other complex cases the role of the minister is not easy to interpret. I first encouraged her to return to Seattle, some 30 miles away. This meant that I would be the one to give her a ride home since she was without funds and it was the middle of the night. When she agreed with this plan of action I walked her to my car and we started driving north on the freeway. After I was up to my normal highway speed she started talking about jumping out of the car. I slowed down, stopped on the shoulder of the road and let her calm down before resuming the trip.

This young woman had a very good memory for addresses and directions. I was getting detailed information from her about how to get to her place. I also introduced the issue of other options. She said that a hospital 10 miles beyond her home had admitted her in the past. We drove past her normal turnoff, heading for this hospital at her request. It was now 4:30 a.m.

In the waiting room of this second hospital only one other person shared the facility at this hour of the evening/morning. This other person was an elderly man who was waiting for word about his wife. She had suffered a heart attack that night. I sat with Jill in the waiting area. When she was paged to report for an exam she insited that I go with her. I walked with her back to the examination room and waited with her until the physician on duty entered the room. Then I stepped outside, returning after the exam to wait with her for the decision. A call was made to the psychiatrist in residence. They decided to admit Jill. When she picked up her bag to leave the exam area I noticed a large Bible on top of other personal items. I left her with a word of blessing before driving home in the early morning dawn.

Worried About An AIDS Test

I had chatted with Rick in an all-night restaurant in Tacoma on many other occasions. When I sat down next to him this

Some authors who have written about suicide have discussed biological factors. One theory, for example, held that a genetic factor explained a run of suicides in a single family. Studies of twins one of whom had committed suicide found no support for such a factor. Another direction for research using biological factors has been the attempt to isolate biochemical variables related to depression and ultimately to suicide but this research has not produced definitive results.

One of the major problems in the study of suicide has been the lack of solid data. Considerably more work is needed by social scientists. The advantage of basic research is that it can be replicated and theory refined or modified accordingly. I would like to see more interest in the special problems of suicide for the street populations I encounter at night.

Understanding Suicide From a Clinical Perspective

A Psycho-Dynamic Approach

Some professionals working regularly with suicidal patients use approaches based upon a sensitivity to the underlying emotins and self-concepts motivating people. From this perspective, followed for example by Kim Smith, considerable emphasis is placed upon such characteristics of high risk attempters as: the tendency to hold feelings inside, not telling others when one hurts and high expectations of self. Now we are talking about specific factors useful when relating to someone who is at risk for suicide. Dr. Smith helps people express their feelings as one way to reduce the risk. People at high risk for attempting suicide are often individuals who take themselves very seriously. These people expect to achieve, they always work and struggle, getting angry at limits. A particularly high-risk person would be the child in a family with high expectations who does not live up to these expectations.

Another part of the psychological pattern discussed in relation to suicide is the tendency to have high expectations of other people. If others are expected never to make a mistake, the mistakes in real life can be shattering. Adolescents are especially prone to feel hurt when someone lets them down. This may trigger a strong desire to hurt another person in some way. Suicide is one way to hurt someone else. This reaction is especially strong in the case of the loss of a close love relationship in adolescence. Adults seldom understand the intensity of attachments during the teen years. When a boy or girl discovers that a very special love is no longer interested in them this can be truly crushing. One suggestion for parents is to stay in touch with the serious involvements, standing ready to help if a crisis in relationships should develop.

Given the crushing finality of the behavior, it is easy to regard suicide as a single-minded rush to death. But available information suggests that in fact such a person generally has very mixed feelings about ending life. There are thoughts of death but also feelings that death is not something to rush into. The topic becomes a high priority on one hand but on the other hand the person at risk will draw away from an open discussion of it. Some of the best intervention strategies take advantage of the internal conflicts to move the person into a lower risk situation. One such strategy, for example, might be to identify with the person's struggle instead of superimposing all directives from some source external to the person.

Depression can become part of the system of feelings leading to suicide. But depression in itself is not a necessary precursor to suicide. Other factors must be considered including the coping mechanisms used by the individual to manage depression. It is best to consider a pattern of feelings and attitudes, not one isolated emotion. Four factors that together place anyone at greater risk are: 1. The tendency to suppress emotions, 2. High achievement orientation, 3. The inability to release expectations of others and 4. Ambivalent feelings about death.

Suicide is considered when depression turns to hopelessness. In a state of hopelessness that is most traumatic a person senses extreme difficulty in preserving a preferred sense of self and is also caught up in a desire to destroy or hurt a frustrating his wife. I offered to telephone for him. He was not sure he wanted me to do this. But finally he said that maybe this would be a good idea. I called her. She said she would take him back.

It was then my responsibility to offer Ben a ride home, some six miles away from the night spot where I met him. On the way home he said he just had to stop for a cup of coffee. We stopped at an all-night donut shop. Then we continued the drive to his apartment. There was some hesitation on his part when we stopped in front of the building. I then walked with him up the two flights of stairs. The woman who responded to his knock thanked me for bringing her husband home. I followed up on this man, meeting him again by appointment. He did get his job back and at least temporarily he was out of the pit of depression he had drifted into the night we first met.

A Loaded Gun

The neighborhood tavern that includes a fair number of unemployed or marginally employed patrons provides a good setting for late night ministry. I was sitting at the bar in one of these places one evening in Denver when someone came up behind me and said in a low voice that he wanted to talk. I turned to see a native American, his long black hair tied up in a knot at the back of his head with a rubber band. I walked with this man over to a booth in a dark corner of the tavern.

His first question for me was "should I marry my girlfriend?" We talked briefly about this. Then Jonathan started talking about the major reason for his eagerness to talk to me. He said that he had been thinking of "ending it all." To be more specific, he said that he had often taken his gun, placed it on the kitchen table and then thought about shooting his girlfriend and then himself.

Jonathan told me that he was on "downers." He was also having a beer, a potentially dangerous combination. While we talked he reached up to untie the rubber band holding his hair in place. The long, black hair fell below his shoulders. His

37

speech was slow and studied, matching his total actions. While we continued talking this man said that he had a "38 pistol" tucked into his boot right there in the booth. Then he added that he had three cartridges in the gun, one was for his girlfriend, one for himself and one for a third party whom he did not identify.

Knowledge that this man held a loaded gun changed the possible options for me. When he said that he had been a VA patient I made a call to the VA hospital, trying to set up an appointment for him. While I was on the telephone in the tavern some of his friends came by and he left with them. There wasn't a great deal I could do since he had a gun in his possession. This encounter represents a judgment call on my part. A street minister in another program was critical of my actions, telling me that my first response should have been to call 911. All professionals, including ministers, are mandated to report situations of grave danger to people. In this case I had to immediately assess the degree of danger to the person, to myself and to the program as well as the long-term effectiveness of the emergency response system. It was my decision at the time to move on to another place when the man drifted away from me. In retrospect I can say that it was the best decision since there was no murder-suicide.

"I Don't Want To Kill Anyone"

A few years ago one of my regular night spots was an inter-racial cafeteria/tavern in Tacoma. This particular place was known for both violence and drug dealing. It was not unusual for me to witness drug transactions on the premises. In this environment my presence was regarded as something of an enigma. But I was able to minister here. On one of my visits I watched as two men started arguing. They faced each other in an aisle area and shouted threats. Since there had been a shooting only a few days before people sitting near the potential fight this night immediately leaned back away from the line of fire. After some loud threats and arm gestures the two separated.

As I was leaving the premises one of the two combatants motioned to me that he wanted to talk. When I sat down beside James he first asked where he could get a Rosary. We then talked about the need to look to God. Next he told me that he really needed someone to help him through his growing feelings of anger and desire to kill a man. It became my responsibility to deal with thoughts of murder, not the kind of ministerial counseling covered in seminary courses!

An "Old Timer" on Skid Road

A few years ago Howard usually ended the day in an emergency shelter in Seattle. One night after he waited in the long line for a piece of day-old pastry and a small carton of milk he talked with me about what it was like to survive on the city streets as one of the homeless. Howard was 61 years old at the time. He had been part of the transient population for over 20 years. He was not strong enough for regular employment and not old enough for any form of regular state or federal aid. He earned a meager income picking up cans, bottles and other material that he sold for recycling. Howard ate in missions and slept wherever he could. Before the public shelter opened in 1979 he camped out under bridges or bushes in all kinds of weather.

When I talked with him Howard was wearing a clean, brown leather jacket. A silver cross hanging from a thin necklace caught my attention. Howard did not claim loyalty to any one church but spoke at length about his faith and sincere desire to help people.

One of Howard's constant concerns was the need to come up with a small amount of money to cover his personal needs. The business of picking up recyclable material was seen by him as becoming a very difficult way to make money. He told me about the time when wine bottles were abundant and easily converted to money at the rate of a penny a bottle. Back in those days he could buy a decent breakfast for 35 cents. When I met him Howard's working day often began around 5:00 a.m. and sometimes did not end until 9:00 p.m. On a slow day he made as little as $5.

Howard had many stories to tell about various sleeping arrangements before his use of the public shelter starting in 1979. He always preferred to stay away from the more popular sleeping places for transients such as the area under the University Street viaduct off First Avenue in downtown Seattle. These places were seen as dangerous by Howard because of their collection of strangers in various stages of drunkenness.

He often walked as far south as the Spokane Street Viaduct to get away from the immediate downtown area at night. The longest period of time he could recall sleeping at one particular place was during the winter of 1978 when he stayed next to a wall not far from the sidewalk near the Downtowner Apartments on Fourth Avenue South. This was his "home" for four and one-half months. The place had two levels for possible sleeping. The most convenient spot was a ledge about two feet wide with an abrupt drop off of about 11 feet to the ground below. One night Howard fell off this ledge during his sleep. The next night he climbed down a tree to the lower level and set up a semi-permanent camp. Sheets of plastic protected him from the rain and held in body heat during the night. He could not be seen from the streets. One day while he was donating his time to help paint a mission building a city engineering crew bulldozed the area, uprooting Howard's tree and hauling away all of his personal property.

As Howard sees life, it is important to try to help others. He makes a special effort to help people with mental or physical disabilities. He also has a high regard for people like Sister Bernie Ternes who have gone out of their way to be responsive to his needs. One night when Howard was climbing down his tree to retire for the night he heard a noise under some near-by bushes. When he looked closer he saw a man in the process of cutting his own throat with a long knife. One slash of the knife had drawn blood but was not fatal. The man was ready to make a deeper cut. Howard hit him on the chin, forcing the knife out of his hand. The stranger ran from the shrubbery. An aid car later picked him up and transported him to the County Hospital. Howard was glad that he prevented the suicide but he was irritated because of the smear of blood on 'his'' wall.

There have also been a number of less dramatic occasions during which Howard has been able to offer assistance to others. On one such occasion he helped a young Chinese couple who parked their car next to his sleeping place. Howard watched as the young man walked toward the parking meter to insert a coin. Before he could deposit money Howard intervened to remind him that it was not necessary to pay for parking at that time of the night. Howard also told the couple that they did not need to worry about their car while they were away. He said that he would look after it personally to make sure that no one broke into it. The couple were very impressed by Howard's generous concern for them. When they returned several hours later, they called Howard up from his sleeping space and presented him with some special items of Chinese food and a dollar bill. This expression of gratitude was very meaningful to Howard.

One of Howard's major complaints about local missions was that they are run on an inflexibly rigid schedule. As he tells it, if you are not there at a certain time you will not be given a meal, lodging or whatever you may be needing. He is very critical of one of the large missions for being overly concerned about money while not ''really'' being interested in people. As he puts it, the real ''heart'' concern ends when you enter a mission. On one occasion he gave hours of his time to help a mission but a few days later when he was hungry he was forced to wait three hours to get a loaf of bread. He also objects to the routine of being forced to sign an agreement that he will not hold a mission responsible for injury on the job when he is giving his time to them.

Howard has considerable perspective on missions because he has seen many of them over the years. A number of years ago he went on occasion to a place called the Jericho Mission. This was located near First Avenue and Washington Street. Howard's memory of the place includes a recollection of prolonged religious services. These services often extended from 7:00 p.m. to 11:00 p.m. as the minister asked different "Sisters" and "Brothers" to give their testimony. Howard feels that the street people were asked to go through too much "ear banging" just to get a night's lodging. At the time there were flop houses where a bed could be purchased for 35 or 50 cents a night. But some of these places were operated by drunks and were so dark or so crawling with bugs that Howard did not feel comfortable sleeping in them.

Howard also remembers a mission run by "Sister" Dorothy years ago. It was across the street from the main fire station. Sister Dorothy must have been a formidable sight on Seattle's Skid Road. Howard describes her as being a big woman, standing nearly six feet tall and weighing in excess of 200 pounds. Her physical bulk was accentuated by her strong authoritarian personality. Sister Dorothy demanded that the men coming to her mission sing during the service and also that no one fall asleep during a service. Any sign of violating her rules resulted in the violator being immediately thrown out of the mission. One night when Howard was at this mission a man went back for a second serving of food during the evening meal. When he later began to show signs that he would not be able to clean up his plate Sister Dorothy came up behind him and pushed his face down into the food. As Howard recalls events, Sister Dorothy was arrested several times by the police for her brutal treatment of the men who came to her mission.

Howard also recalls a unique kind of mission activity on Seattle's streets in the past. On Occidental Avenue a shapely young woman called Sister Faye and an attractive female partner played the tambourine and sang gospel songs. Men on the street were more attracted by the physical appearance of these two women than by their attempts at evangelism.

When these tambourine players collected a small amount of money they took a short break, going down the street to one of the taverns where they purchased drinks of wine to help fortify themselves for another round of music making on the street.

On Occidental Street there was also a mission known as "The Cheese Mission." For Howard the best part of this mission was that religious services were always short. The operator of the mission simply read the 23rd Psalm. Each man was given a piece of cheese and a slice of bread. During the 1960s a bed for the night could be purchased for 25 cents.

Howard shares the serious concerns of many old timers about the changing degree of personal safety on the downtown streets. As he views the situation, there was a time when the streets were safe at any time of the day or night. Today he feels that there are too many "crazy" people around who regularly carry switch blade knives or other dangerous weapons. One night while he was waiting for the street traffic to clear so that he could climb down his tree in privacy, two young men approached him and asked for money. He told them that he did not have any. One of the men picked up a stick and hit him on the right side of the head, knocking him to the ground. His glasses broke in the fall. Fortunately, a car appeared and the occupants of this car shouted at the young man to "leave that old man alone." The two youths ran off. Howard claims that such a direct physical attack without provocation would have been unheard of on the streets of Skid Road long ago.

Howard also sees major changes in the sale of sex on the downtown streets. Years ago there were few street prostitutes in or near Skid Road. Most hotels were for single men. The rooms were often spacious and reasonably priced. A few hotels were for men and women. Some of these latter places became places where hookers worked. The Morrison Hotel where the City's Emergency Shelter is now located was one such place. The Old Seattle Hotel which is now a parking garage was another. These places were well known on the street. There was no need for the hasty arrangements on the sidewalk or the clandestine manipulations involving high priced call girls which characterize sex for sale in downtown Seattle today. Howard's comments should not be taken as the final word on the condition of downtown missions. Today there is considerable variety in the quality of programs operated by these facilities. With the sharp escalation in land values downtown missions now have major difficulty maintaining a presence.

Discussion

There is no substitude for direct, personal encounters with individuals as a way to understand late-night, downtown ministry. Operation Nightwatch in Seattle has now touched individuals with caring for over twenty years. This unique ministry has also been extended to other cities as reported in the pages of this chapter and in subsequent chapters.

Today most cities have an array of services for the homeless, the chemically dependent and others. But often a personal touch is missing, especially late at night. In the Gospels Jesus is most often pictured as a street minister, walking with people in need. Operation Nightwatch and other forms of contemporary street ministry are an extension of our Lord's work.

It is very hard to communicate the intensity that can surface in a chance meeting with a stranger. This chapter has attempted to give at least some sense of such encounters. Other programs point to numbers and/or financial data as signs of success. In our work success is interpreted in terms of countless encounters that can become major points of personal change. The remaining chapters in this part of the book continue the sharing of late-night encounters arranged under specific topics plus information helpful in a review of possible responses to problems.

Chapter 2
Down and Out

Few of us are far from the sights and smells of homelessness and poverty in general. My experiences include work with "drifters" who wandered through a small town looking for a handout from the local church, extensive contacts with the homeless of different cities plus individual struggles around the experience of being unemployed while trying to start a program of street ministry. The urgency of the topic is reinforced for me by the sight of people stretched out on the lawn and front steps of a big city church two blocks away from the small room where these pages are being written in rough draft. These people have slept in their respective locations throughout the night. In the city poverty and/or the threat of poverty can be overwhelming.

Background

Homelessness

Political processes and psychological defense mechanisms make it difficult to look at homelessness objectively. Civic leaders minimize the problem, fearful of creating an image harmful to downtown business interests. Sometimes programs that promise to rid the streets of the homeless give little concern to the ultimate plight of these people. Anyone who has ever had the experience of sitting in a street level restaurant while a haggard, hungry looking person stands outside begging can appreciate why people build up psychological defenses to keep them from being constantly pulled into the hopelessness of homelessness. In a place like New York City open hostility develops between aggressive "street people" and others.

Accurate estimates of the extent of homelessness in America are difficult to obtain. Beth Spring, writing in *Christianity Today*, (1989) mentions estimates of from 350,000 to three million. She also reports projections of as many as eighteen million in America by the turn of the century. Agencies in daily contact with the homeless are often strained beyond their ability to respond. Until recently Seattle's Operation Nightwatch maintained a few cheap hotel rooms for transients. The program continues to be the primary late-night referral resource for the city. Some nights 20 to 30 or more people who request shelter are turned down. No space is available in the city. Other cities face similar shortages of emergency housing. The Hollywood district of Los Angeles, for example, has limited emergency beds for homeless youth. On any given night teens can be seen begging on Hollywood Boulevard. Some will explain that they are "on the waiting list" for a bed in one of the local shelters.

One way to avoid action around a problem is to always see that problem as so large that nothing can really be done. Talk of "thousands" of homeless people may not translate into practical help for the few hard-core homeless one sees every day if he works downtown. I am thinking of a man who lives on Hollywood Boulevard. He wears a tattered brown/black overcoat. His face is weathered and aged beyond his years. He has not washed in weeks, maybe months. This man's most obvious feature is his feet. Both feet protrude naked from a pair of out-sized sandals. The toes on these feet have lost their individual identity. They are merged into swollen, red, hideous clubs of cracked skin.

This man can not lift his swollen feet more than a few inches off the ground. He shuffles from place to place, spending most of his time sitting on public benches. One night I decided to approach him. When I walked to within a few yards of him he started yelling at me to keep my distance. He is dying on the street in front of hundreds of people who pass him every day and night. Surely some kind of involuntary commitment would be more humane than his present state. By his obvious presence this one man reinforces the agony of homelessness far beyond what would be expected for one individual.

In addition to realistic responses to real people we also need a better understanding of the different kinds of folks who are "homeless." I am writing this chapter in Hollywood, California. This setting makes me aware of the children and teens who are homeless. In one block along Hollywood Boulevard this morning I was approached by three teenagers, all pleading for money, all homeless. Hollywood has become a mecca for homeless youth. But no city is immune from this aspect of homelessness. Teenagers can become professional in the survival techniques of the street. Agencies in Hollywood strongly advise people not to reinforce the begging on the streets. Youth can find formal help systems. They are, of course, vulnerable to all of the dangers of life on the city street.

Over the years the homeless youth of the city have changed in many ways. Today's teenager living on the streets is more likely to be a "throw-away" kid than in years passed. One example of such a teenager is an 18-year-old I met late one night on a street just off Hollywood Bouelvard. I was drawn to this fellow by the sight of black/blue and swollen tissue under his eyes. He was sitting on a bench outside a restaurant. I sat beside him and we talked for some time.

This young man needed to share his feelings around the experience of being severely beaten two days before our encounter. In his account of the beating I was told that three friends attacked him because he threatened to become an informer about their credit card scam and car theft business. Richard was beaten and cut with a knife. He told me that the emergency medical personnel who attended him informed him that he was lucky to be alive. His attackers had a gun. The gun was pointed at him. But they decided to beat him up instead. In the process his long hair was cut, a severe loss to this youth who was proud of his "hard rock" entertainer appearance which included shoulder length hair.

This 18-year-old had no home in Hollywood. He said that he had been in the city for one month. During that time he developed a friendship network of some 100 people. He was forced to leave his home in the mid-West when he was 13 years old. His parents could not handle what they described as destructive behavior. He was labeled an alcoholic and psychotic. After spending some time with relatives, Richard roamed from city to city.

Some of the homeless are alcohol/drug addicted and/or mentally ill. It is most unfortunate that all of these people are often placed in a simplistic, homogeneous category. Specialized efforts are needed in response to the mentally ill and the chemically dependent. When such chronic problems are present the process of providing emergency shelter becomes much more complicated than some groups are willing to recognize. Occasionally I hear well intended people saying that they want to open their church as a shelter. I applaud the concern but encourage a serious exploration of the problems.

The youth, alcohol/drug addicted and mentally ill are only the most obvious groups of people included as part of today's homeless scene. It is more difficult to categorize people such as the women who are popularly labeled as "shopping bag ladies." These women may be both elderly and mentally ill. Their age and lifestyle recommend special considerations. From my experience with the homeless at night I see the need for a half-way house for these older women of the street. They are eligible for Social Security or SSI. It should not be necessary for them to forage on the city streets. But confusion, the cutting of social ties and other factors serve to hold them in the round of bare existence which they share with others who are homeless. The most recent change in the population of the homeless is the increase in the number of people staying in shelters who are working part or fulltime. They do not earn enough to pay for housing.

In the past the mission represented the only local resource for the homeless. The traditional mission was and is planned primarily with men in mind. As the name implies, a mission often places strong emphasis upon spirituality. In addition to the church sponsored mission there are now city operated emergency shelters and shelters run by religious organizations that do not place high emphasis upon formal religious services.

One of my concerns is the need to help folks assume as much independence as they are capable of. This requires a program offering counseling, job training/placement and other needed services. Some agencies have gone too far in reacting against what they consider "force feeding" of religion. One agency, for example, prohibits any form of counseling on the premises. Transients are given a bed, no questions asked. Many of those served by this shelter have serious psychological problems. In contrast to this approach most cities now have strong programs planned to bridge the distance between the condition of being homeless to that of having a regular place of residence and/or some kind of employment.

Underemployment

When I speak to groups about the kinds of problems we see in late-night ministry I try to move from homelessness to problems of poverty in general. Homelessness can pull on the emotions because it is so visible. But there are hidden forms of poverty that are both more pervasive and more difficult to address than homelessness. Underemployment is one of these aspects of poverty that does not receive enough attention.

In street ministry I have seen many people who are working and living at a regular address but who are not getting enough money to really get by. The bartenders in a Skid Road tavern or blue collar, neighborhood tavern often make very little money. Many of these bartenders are women. Contrary to popular belief they seldom make money on the side through illicit sex. Most are very middle-aged. They have limited work skills. Perhaps a husband died or the husband is working at another low-paying job. The bartending is part of the minimal income package for the family. The hours are long. There is no medical insurance coverage for this high-stress work.

In the next section of this chapter the "personal glimpses" include reference to a man who sells newspapers. He would not be included in a survery of the homeless. But he is part of the larger picture of poverty in America. He does not make enough money to pay for an apartment, food and clothes. He seldom gets a time of uninterrupted sleep as he sits dozing off at odd hours in the lobby of an old, downtown hotel.

When fast food places hire people part time as a way to cut expenses and do not cover such basics as health insurance this also adds to the burden of individual poverty. In St. Louis the director of a program for female prostitutes shared some of her problems with me. One of her major concerns is the need to place women in regular employment, away from the life on the street. This is made more difficult by the combination of low-pay and short hours in fast food places. These places are the most accessible sources of employment for women who are trying to re-enter the job market. But the salary is so low that the women are tempted to turn again to the more profitable work of prostitution.

Senior citizens on meager, fixed incomes are also part of the often neglected forms of poverty in America. Individuals with incomes less than $400 a month find it very hard to survive. Any kind of crisis can be an unsurmountable wall for these people. The severity of the problem depends in part on where the person happens to live. In Los Angeles even the cheapest kind of rental often demands deposits of $800 or more. With a sub-standard, fixed income a senior citizen always lives close to the street.

Unemployment

It is hard to get good data on the numbers of people who are homeless. Although unemployment rates are quoted often it is also difficult to know how many people are able to work and looking for work but unable to find it. After employment

50

benefits have been exhausted people can become lost to the record keeping system.

Homelessness merits more attention. But helping agencies and the church must also be more responsive to the experience of unemployment and other temporary or long-term financial dislocations. With the stress of large mortgage payments and normal middle-class expectations a suburbanite who becomes unemployed may experience much more stress than someone for whom homelessness has become a way of life. Suicide risk is much greater in those cases where there has been a temporary, major reduction in income.

There is no simple, definitive book on homelessness/poverty in America today. The topic is very complex. One way to gain some insight is to listen to people who have walked among the homeless and the poor. I have had some opportunity to do this in recent years. I share some of my experiences in the pages which follow.

Personal Glimpses

A Room at the YMCA

I have indicated that the first draft of this chapter was written in Hollywood. More specifically, the writing was done in a room at the Hollywood YMCA. Staying in this facility gives me another personal glimpse into one part of the homeless/poverty scene. The building is used as one of the places where homeless youth are referred by service agencies. My room at the Y is small, only nine feet by 12 feet. There is a strange odor in the room. The ceiling tiles are broken and appear to be ready to fall down. An old Zenith TV sits on a rusted metal brace which juts out from one wall. All of the knobs of this ancient TV set are broken. The room has no bath room facilities. These facilities are down the hall. The combination toilet/shower area is cluttered with toilet paper.

One toilet runs constantly. The room rents for $25 a night, a bargain in the Hollywood district.

A person who has never stayed in such a facility may find it hard to imagine how lifestyle might change while living there. Of course there is concern for personal safety and the possibility of theft. One afternoon I overheard a fellow resident of the Y complain about the disappearance of $110. He was told that he should walk to the police station to make a report since they would not respond if he simply called by phone. I tried not to leave anything of value in the room. It was easy to keep money and credit cards on my person. But I also had items such as a small travel iron, a film on Operation Nightwatch and clothes which would have been difficult to replace.

In this type of housing the minor comforts one might expect are not present. There is no air conditioning. Street sounds come in through open windows. One night someone pulled the fire alarm as a prank. This sound cut through the darkness for a long time before it was turned off. Each room gets one medium sized bath towel. There are no hand towels and no bar soap. One morning while I was shaving in the communal washroom a friendly cockroach joined me in the experience. On another morning two other residents were washing their clothes in sinks next to me as I was shaving and drying my hair. This facility does not lend itself to high inspiration.

After staying in the cheap room at the YMCA on Saturday night I attended a Sunday School class and church service at one of the large churches in Hollywood on Sunday morning. The experiences at church stood out in sharp contrast to the experience of living in a sub-standard room. The Sunday School class was a trip into words and ideas. There was no touching of practical issues. I wondered what a person with limited resources would gain from a philosophical discussion of religious life. As I sat in a pew by myself during the worship service I glanced down to see a small bug crawling along my arm. I immediately wondered if I was getting body lice from my sleeping arrangement. It was easy for me to see again how far removed some of the formal worship exercises are from the major concerns of the poor.

No Money and No Hope

Another way to get a personal glimpse of abject poverty is to look closely into the faces of the poor. I still remember one man in particular on the street in downtown St. Louis. It was one of the big celebration nights during the 4th of July when the waterfront area is bright with happy crowds of revelers. Not far from this carnival atmosphere I encountered a man sitting on a concrete stoop along the sidewalk. A large bag was propped up near him.

I stopped to chat with this stranger. He had very little to say. I did learn that the plastic bag was full of soda cans. He had been collecting these cans all day. But city clean up crews were on the scene before him so his efforts produced only one bag full of cans. I asked this man how much he expected to get for these cans. He said "about $1.50." I gave him $1.00 to nearly double his earnings for the day. The most impressive part of this experience for me was the reaction on the part of this stranger to my gift. He gave no emotional response. He was so dejected that any addition to his meager resources just did not register. There was no word of thanks. His was a bare survival existence. There was no energy for emotional exchanges.

It is the look of the person who begs for money that gets to me. Some are professional panhandlers. Others are simply trying to survive during a temporary crisis. Ragged clothes and that look of utter dejection speak very loudly on the personal level. As one may imagine, this places the whole issue in a very different context than one would get from only waching homeless scenes from a safe distance on TV or reading about the problem in the daily newspaper.

"I'm No Good"

In Portland, Oregon I occasionally walked across the Burnside Street Bridge away from the downtown area to talk with people as they lined up to get into an emergency shelter. One night I was pulled into a conversation with Paul, a man in his mid 50s. He seemed very anxious. That day he had looked for work. He said that he had looked for a dishwashing job or for "any kind of work." But he found nothing. The only thing he had to show for his efforts was a painful display of blisters on both feet.

As I talked with Paul another man came along and sat down beside us. This other man was several years older than Paul. At the sight of this third person, Paul spoke again of his plight including his view of his own worth. He informed me that he was "no g . . d . . good, no good for nothing." Then he turned to the older man, pointed a finger at him and said "that guy gets a Social Security check, he is worth something. I ain't worth nothing to nobody." This estimation of self-worth is one of the most devastating aspects of chronic unemployment or underemployment.

Drinking Black Coffee at 1:00 a.m.

As I have indicated, underemployment is a more extensive problem than homelessness. When I think of underemployment I always think of Sam, a 61-year-old fellow I saw many times in downtown St. Louis. He can often be seen sitting in an all-night cafeteria. A cup of black coffee is on the table in front of him. But late at night or early in the morning Sam is most likely to be nodding in a semi-sleep state instead of actually drinking the coffee. Some years before I met him Sam was laid off after working for the same company for 25 years. The company had no retirement plan. Sam first exhausted all of his unemployment compensation and then started selling newspapers. As he explained to me, dishwashing at minimal wages for a few hours a week does not pay as much as selling papers.

Sam is one example of many folks who are working but not making enough to get by on. For him the working day begins at 2:00 a.m. when he is the first in line to pick up newspapers. His major selling time is between 6:00 a.m. and 8:00 a.m. when he covers some of the downtown office buildings. During the middle part of the day he gets some rest. He starts selling again around 10:00 p.m. To boost his income he sells his blood for plasma twice a week. All of his efforts do not net him enough to pay for a regular place to sleep. One of his personal goals is to make enough money each week to stay in a cheap hotel over the weekend.

Sam is a rugged individualist. He refuses to go to emergency shelters because, according to him, these places have "body lice and lots of fights." He also tries not to go for free food because he feels that this might deprive someone who is more needy. Sam is very bitter about people who get temporary help for such items as a fan or a heater for an apartment and then sell these items to buy "beer or a joint."

The daily schedule for Sam is a little like the tiring routine of a shopping bag lady. He seldom gets a regular period of unbroken sleep. When he has money he goes to places where he can eat all he wants for a set price. He drinks a lot of coffee and dreams of the time when he will be able to draw Social Security payments. As one might imagine, Sam is vulnerable to all of the dangers of the street. Two years ago he had a car and used it to sleep in. One night two men approached this car from either side with drawn guns. They took Sam's money but left him when he refused to crawl into the trunk of the car. Sam has had four other occasions when he has been robbed during the last four years on the street. One of these affairs included a frightful encounter with two youths who first took his money and then said they they were going to shoot him. Sam pleaded with them, asking why they wanted to kill him since they had all of his money. One of the two explained that he "just wanted to kill somebody." Fortunately, someone came along the street and the two youths ran away.

Staying in a Skid Road Hotel

As I have indicated, this chapter was written in rough draft while I was staying for a week in the Hollywood YMCA. This was not my first experience with sub-standard housing. A few years ago while working to get Portland's Operation Nightwatch started I decided to stay in a regular Skid Road hotel to better understand some of the people I was trying to help. A temporary trip into the world of the poor is not the same as being trapped in that pattern. But even a short exposure can help one gain new insights into a world which he may have little personal experience with.

In the hotel where I stayed rooms rented for $90 a month. I paid $4.00 a night plus $1.00 for a key deposit. The rooms were small, containing only a single bed, one metal folding chair and an old dresser. As I climbed the stairs to my room on the second floor I was stung by the putrid odor of the place. When I turned on the bare overhead light in my room cockroaches scurried across the walls. There was no curtain on the single window. All of the people on this floor used a common toilet and shower facility which was a distance down the hall from my room.

One advantage for a minister in such a place is that the opportunity for serving others is always close at hand. After dressing for work on the street I left my room and started down the hall. I was stopped by two of my neighbors. One of these men was sitting on the floor in front of the door to his room. He was too drunk to manage the process of unlocking his own door. I turned the key for him and helped him into the room where he fell into his bed.

On the street that night I happened to run into one of the old timers who lives in the neighborhood. When I told him where I was staying he immediately pulled a small canister of mace from an inside coat pocket and offered it to me for self-protection. He then lectured me at some length on the problems of personal safety. According to him a man was shot in the hotel where I was staying just the night before. A resident of the hotel thought that someone was trying to break into his room and fired through the closed door. In another recent episode of violence described by my new friend an elderly man was beaten and robbed in the doorway of one of the other cheap hotels near my hotel. This man's chest was kicked in. When his attackers could not find anything of value on his person they forced silver braces out of his mouth in their zeal for anything of value. I was learning first hand that one of the major concerns of the poor in the city is the ever-present fear of physical violence.

On that particular evening I returned late to the hotel. As I walked up the stairs I saw a bloody mass on the landing between floors. This was not clear blood from a flesh wound. Perhaps it was matted, bloody material which had been coughed up from an internal hemorrhage. Internal bleeding is one of the painful and potentially lethal results sometimes seen in the late stages of alcoholism. Before undressing in the room I draped some of my extra clothes over the bare window as a makeshift curtain. I crawled in under the sheet and single blanket. The room was warm. A peaceful feeling came over me. I felt that this was where I should be at the time. I fell asleep without too much difficulty. In the early hours of the morning I was awakened by the eerie sound of a fire alarm. This sound, coming from a neary-by building blared out for about two hours before the night again became silent. I had placed the single metal folding chair under the door knob before going to bed as an added safety precaution. In the morning I opened this chair, knelt down on the bare floor beside my bed in that $4.00 room and thanked God for the opportunity of Christian service.

On the next occasion I had to stay in that Skid Road hotel I came away with new impressions. I was given a different room. This room did not have a mirror over the small sink.

I found one of the hotel employees who loaned me a piece of broken, discarded mirror. I was surprised by the change in the odor of the building. The previous putrid smell came from temporary residents, not from the building itself. The cockroaches in this second room were a sight to behold. When I lifted a wash cloth near the sink they were everywhere.

I was recovering from a viral infection on this second visit to the hotel. Late at night as I lay on my bed in the small room I heard a man coughing down the hall. His was a very deep cough. Since I had just gone through a sick spell during which I had the normal attention one gets from family members, I wondered what it would be like to be sick and all alone. How does a person cope in a situation where there is no one to go for cough syrup, no money for cough syrup and no one to show an interest in his condition? Health and health care are major problems for the poor. I have seen people using walkers on the upper floors of cheap hotels which have no elevators. These people seldom get out of the building. An alcoholic in such a situation must depend on a barter system to get alcohol up the stairs. Any kind of regular monthly check is soon completely spent in such an arrangement.

As one might imagine, there were many ways in which my activities changed because of my residence in that Skid Road hotel. There was nothing in the bare room to interest me. I normally watch the news on TV and relax by watching other network shows. But this room had no TV or radio. I found myself going out on the street much earlier than is my custom in night ministry. Like regular residents of the place, I needed some diversion away from the drabness. On my last Saturday in the place I awoke before 7:00 a.m. and started getting ready for a new day. I had a morning meeting to attend, a bus to catch for my return to Seattle and things to do upon my return home. As I was dressing and packing my suitcase I was suddenly impressed by the silence around me in the hotel. No one else was getting ready for the day. These people had little to get ready for. One of the major deprivations of the poor is in not having something meaningful to do.

Standing in the Unemployment Line

The best way for me to give a personal glimpse of the experience of being unemployed is to share my own experience with the unemployment line a few years ago. In Denver at the downtown Job Service Center the long line of the unemployed forms outside in warm weather and then winds through the basement halls during the cold, winter months. I reported every week for a few weeks and then once a month after the initial reporting period. One of the main reasons for reporting to the Center was to provide a listing of places where I had looked for work. If I went early enough to be one of the first in line the visit took only one or two hours. During this time I had ample opportunity to reflect on the whole scene. I was always reminded that people with average ability or less were working for the State as security guards or interviewers while I was unable to find work. It is not particularly inspiring to start the day's search for work surrounded by people who are drawing unemployment because they cannot find work.

The experience of unemployment for me came after long years of regular work. My work career began in high school at the age of 16 when I held a part-time job while going to school. I managed to find and to keep full-time jobs while completing undergraduate and graduate degrees in college. Immediately prior to the time of unemployment I had held teaching positions on the faculty of different universities for a period of 13 years. This background did not help in the immediate situation of being unemployed. If anything, it made me more discouraged when I realized that people with specific job skills were more likely to find work than I was.

During the time of drawing unemployment I became very disillusioned about the whole process. One of the disturbing realities was that there was very little connection between the formal demands of the Job Service Center and the actual process of getting a job. Special employment "counselors" at the Center were no help whatsoever. They simply flipped through a microfiche listing of job openings and then signed one of many cards for continuing eligibility. The weekly reporting of places where I had looked for work was often a crude formality. I wrote down places where I dropped by just for the purpose of putting something on the form. The actual job search was done apart from the bureaucratic system of the Job Service Center.

Another disturbing part of the whole experience was what it was doing within the family. There were few opportunities to express feelings around being unemployed. At times there was a deliberate avoidance of the topic. It was a difficult situation for the extended family members to relate to in any meaningful way. There was no financial sharing in the family during the time of unemployment.

In contacts with family members, friends and people in the church it was often the small things that became very important to me. When someone openly expressed concern this was always appreciated. I attended church every Sunday during those difficult months but never heard a sermon that was particularly helpful in the specific area of being unemployed. One sermon was, in fact, a very negative experience for me. The minister went on at some length about his own comfortable security. He spoke about his fireplace, his large back yard and his pets. I thought about my own problems in paying the rent on a small apartment. During this worship service and at other times I was hounded by the question "Why me?" While going through this difficult time I gave two nights a week in volunteer service to the downtown Denver night community in street ministry.

In thinking back about this period of my life I recall how devastating it was for me. My sense of self-worth was eroded. I was reminded daily of the reality that our society values people according to their respective place in the world of work. Other people my age were going to work. I had no job. I was out of place. I over-reacted to small insults to my ego. At the time I was staying near a private Univeristy that our two children had graduated from. One day I decided to spend a little time in the college library. But when I tried to get in I was told to produce some evidence of student or faculty status. When I was turned away from the welcome sight of stacks of library books I was both furious at the system and challenged again in terms of my personal worth. Although it has now been years since those dark days I am still hounded both by a degree of insecurity and by problems in looking too much at what others have in comparison to me.

Responses

Many different specific responses to homelessness and poverty in general are needed. One important area of response includes the considerable work now going on to build the kind of society in which these problems are less likely to occur. There must be focused attention on the problems of high-risk groups such as the single-parent family and the elderly. On the individual level everyone can help by doing all he/she can to ensure that they do not become part of the problem. The process of training for a career and making choices around job changes demand the best thinking. But with strong advocacy for societal changes and the best of personal planning there will always be a need to intervene directly with the homeless/poor. The one-to-one response is the highest priority for street ministry.

Being There

It is important to share the turf with those who are poor and/or homeless. One of the areas of greatest loss for the poor is the loss of a feeling of self-worth coupled with low levels or no contact with people who are not in a similar plight. As I write this I am keenly aware of the great discrepancy between the honest needs of people and the availability of solid resources. Sometimes I feel there is very little I can do for a stranger in desperate circumstances. One thing I can give is my presence and my concern. I know that this is never enough. But it is a start. We need to walk with others in their pain and loss.

This deliberate response of "being there" is important for many different kinds of economic dislocation. A counselor working with the unemployed shared his list of the most important needs of the unemployed with me. At the top of this list is "the need to be heard." People who have lost a job and people who are homeless on the city streets need to have someone who will listen. This calls for a ministry of presence. Providing for tangible needs is important but this never takes the place of personal contact.

It takes skill to be effective in a support network for someone going through an experience like unemployment. Friends are important but the quality of a network is not necessarily measured in terms of numbers. Sociologists Kathryn Ratcliff-Strother and Janet Bogdan (1988), for example, discuss problems women encounter when going through a time of unemployment. Some friends try to be helpful but only add to the problem. They may look at women's work only from the perspective of economics, saying that since the husband is working the wife shouldn't worry so much. This view ignores the larger issue of what the work might mean for the woman's sense of self. In this and other situations one important strategy is to gain a better sense of how the problem is viewed by the person involved.

Spiritual Counsel

Jesus saw His commission as directly related to the process of preaching good tidings to the poor. Those of us in ministry today would do well to follow His sense of destiny as clearly outlined by His Selection of Scripture to interpret ministry:

The Spirit of the Lord is upon me,
Because he anointed me to preach

good tidings to the poor:
He has sent me to proclaim
release to the captives,
And recovery of sight to the
blind.
To set at liberty them that are
bruised,
To proclaim the acceptable year of
the Lord (Luke 4:18-19, RSV).

There is no calling higher than the challenge to preach the gospel. This commission is in sharpest focus when applied directly to the poor and those in different kinds of bondage. The experience of special annointing seldom comes with winged angels present on a mountain top. It comes out of the process of continuing to work when budgets are low, when committees hassle needlessly over minutia and when it seems that few are really interested in things of the Spirit. "Spiritual counsel" is always a two-way street. I am often blessed by strangers as I reach out on the dark streets of the city.

I have seen many different kinds of spiritual counseling on the city streets. One evening on Hollywood Boulevard I witnessed gospel teams preaching on the street, teams passing out religious tracts, a man carrying a huge wooden cross, a group of chanting Hare Krishnas and vigorous evangelism by Scientology adherents.

Sometimes people are approached as if they were untouchable. The preacher may not really want to get close. Literature is handed out at arms length. When there is dialogue it is a one-way delivery of a "sermon" to "sinners." Do we dare touch lepers? Can we embrace a man or woman who is shabbily dressed but desperately in need of a human touch? Maybe the real problem for the church today is not "out there" but instead the very difficult task of touching our own hidden frustrations, fears, guilt and lack of faith. Jesus touched lepers. His church must take a new look at the unlovely, the untouchable, the unholy. It is in redeeming the leper in ourselves and in others that we become the true messengers of Divine love.

When ministry proceeds at a distance from the real person problems always result. On the street this can result in life-threatening situations because the person is in effect ignored as over-zealous evangelists hover around a narrow concept of what is spiritual. One evening when I was working on the street in Portland, Oregon I became involved in a number of intense exchanges. Late that evening I met three men who formed a small gospel team for street preaching. When they saw my clergy collar they felt moved to tell me about one of their experiences that night. They said that they had found a stranger who was bleeding from a fresh knife wound in the neck. They went on to report that their response to this crisis was to form a circle around the bleeding man and to pray for him. They said that they ''really felt power'' in that prayer. My only thought was that I would want them to first call for emergency medical aid if they shoud find me in a similar condition. There are times to pray and times to take other action. Those who define spiritual work in narrow terms as preaching and passing out literature are seldom prepared to look seriously at the whole person. They too often start from a perspective of alienation as if they are at battle against people instead of relating to the guilt, sin and nobility which can be found in everyone.

In touching lepers one soon learns that things making a person untouchable in the eyes of society do not necessarily make that person untouchable in the sight of God. I have been reminded of this many times. One day, for example, I walked past a long line of men waiting for a shelter to open late in the afternoon. A man waiting in this line repeated the Lord's prayer for my benefit in German. Another man who was stretched out under a blanket on the sidewalk was reading a Bible.

Spiritual counsel does not need to follow a pre-set, stereotyped pattern of response. Often the attitude and shared feelings are more important than words. It is altogether too easy for spiritual counseling to take on the methods of secular society. Religion is often commercialized. People are reinforced for the process of shouting at strangers, yelling about hell and damnation. For some any form of printed message becomes a fetish. It is as if eternal credits are earned by littering city streets with pamphlets that shop owners or the city engineering crew must sweep up the next day. The real need is for people to give themselves to others. Giving of ourselves at a deep level, sharing at points of honest need and high sincerity are central for spiritual counsel.

Giving Practical Assistance

In street ministry there are many opportunities to give in very practical ways to others. People often think only of giving money. Money is seldom given out on the street by seasoned street ministers. But there are many other practical things which are done in the spirit of ministry. I have often given people a ride late at night, for example. In St. Louis I regularly transported homeless strangers to local shelters. I also gave rides to poor folks who were stranded a long way from home at the City Hospital. Sometimes my greatest contribution to a night person is to give information about local shelters or free food options in the city.

On one occasion I took a man who had been staying in an emergency shelter for a job interview. This man was trained as a truck driver. We went some distance out of the downtown area for his interview. He was very middle-aged and walked with a noticeable limp from an old injury to his left leg. I waited while he took the formal exam. I became a little anxious for him when I noticed that younger, able-bodied men were also applying for the job. After the written exam my friend pulled himself up into a tractor rig for a road test. He turned that powerful tractor around "on a dime," quickly demonstrating his driving skill. I was happy for him when he was told that he had the job. He was hired on the spot. I drove back downtown alone and never saw the man again.

Begging has become commonplace in most American cities. This behavior often triggers strong reactionary responses. Seattle, Washington and other cities have either passed ordinances against "aggressive panhandling" or initiated strong informal controls. But downtown remains a place where the daily sights include windshield washing panhandlers, sign carrying street people and those who position themselves in strategic places on the sidewalk to take full advantage of the flow of pedestrian traffic.

A very small percentage of those who ask for money perpetuate a distorted image of this behavior because of the way they work the system. In Los Angeles, for example, a couple were arrested after reports of a scam they were operating in supermarket parking lots and service stations. One of their standard lines was that the woman was pregnant and that their money had been stolen. Reportedly this couple collected as much as $200 an hour from unsuspecting people who willingly contributed to their cause.

The few who get rich by panhandling are not representative of the vast majority of those who stand on the sidewalks of the city in all kinds of weather asking for a quarter or a dollar. These people are seldom regarded as part of the positive image of downtown. They may be blamed for the exodus of shoppers from downtown to suburban malls. I have indicated that I seldom give money at night. It would be dangerous to carry large sums of money and/or to be identified as someone who routinely hands out money. For me it is more important to relate on other dimensions. But I also see the problem from the view of the person on the street. The code of the homeless calls for a sharing of resources. If I am always unresponsive to even the smallest request I run the risk of appearing calloused to practical needs, interested only in the "soul."

Anyone who walks the downtown streets on a regular basis has developed his own strategy about how to respond to panhandling. One message in the content of this chapter is that sometimes it is possible to become acquainted with a stranger. If one can get beyond the faceless anonymity of a contact he can be of much greater help. Sometimes the reflexive donation of a quarter becomes a way to say "leave me alone." It is not easy to respond to expressions of need when one knows very little about another. I can share a couple of examples of how I have seen the process of caring work on the streets of the city.

Early in this chapter I made a passing reference to a man who stumbles along Hollywood Boulevard, his swollen feet and filthy appearance making a very repulsive sight. I said that I felt sorry for him and tried to talk to him. But be became so angry when I walked toward him that I had to back off. Although I was never able to help him others did get involved. One night while talking with one of the professional mimes for the Hollywood Wax Museum when he was taking a break I was given more insight into the man with the swollen feet. It seems that at one time he was a successful attorney. His wife was murdered and this threw him into a state of total confusion from which he never recovered. The mime took the first step by coming up with this personal background on the man who was a total stranger to me.

The involvement of the mime did not stop there. He too had observed that the older man lived by sorting through garbage containers. So the mime waited until the man made his way to the sidewalk in front of McDonald's. Then he went inside, purchased a Big Mac, french fries and a soft drink, asking the cashier to place the food in a sack. Next the mime took this sack of food outside and dropped it in a trash container which was on the daily route of the stranger. The old man in rags reached down into the trash to retrieve one of his few complete meals of the day. When one really wants to get involved sometimes it takes ingenuity.

As another example of an unusual way to help, I was impressed by a daily ritual which takes place on a street corner along Hollywood Boulevard. Around 10:00 a.m. two men meet. One is very unkept in appearance, obviously part of the Hollywood homeless population. The other man is fairly well dressed, obviously someone who lives in a near-by house or apartment. The well-dressed man always has something to give to the other man. I have watched as a used coat is given, for example. It is not given at arms length. The one who gives helps the homeless man put the coat on and seems to be genuinely interested in whether or not it fits. Other times I have seen sandwiches handed to the man who has spent the night sleeping outside. I do not know what relationship, if any, these two men have to each other. They could be brothers or total strangers. Since I no longer make the trips to Hollywood I will most likely never know the whole story. But it represents a different way to respond to need than I usually see on the downtown streets. Maybe we need some form of adoption in which one person "adopts" another, trying to find out about this other and tailoring the giving to real need.

These examples of involvement suggest another dilemma, that of maintaining a meaningful boundary between helping deeds and personal life space. A good friend who has also served as a volunteer minister on the streets at night told me that getting too involved to the point of inviting strangers home resulted in the break-up of his marriage. Obviously the precise nature of boundaries will vary from one to another. But some kind of limitations is important. I make it a point to keep my work with people on the streets apart from my own family life. I do not bring strangers home. I do not give out my home telephone number. In times of crisis people can reach me through an answering service. This gives me some control over the late-night contacts.

Telling Others About the Problems

A secondary response to homelessness and poverty coming from street ministry is the process of volunteers telling others about the problems. Clergy can become strong advocates for changes. They can be a major community resource in planning for better intervention strategies and for structural changes in the system. First-hand contact makes it much easier to gain perspective on any problem. Popular issues always engender a degree of myth. There are many myths about homelessness, for example. Recently a city council member in one large American city remarked that the poor are confined in one part of town because of choice. As he put it, "people go there because that is where their friends are. They want to stay in Skid Road." I know very few people living in Skid Road conditions who really desire this lifestyle. One reason people stay in Skid Road is that they know that they are less likely to be picked up by the police in "that" part of town. There are many forces which now perpetuate dire poverty in America. A deliberate look into the face of individuals living on the street does not solve the problem. But it can go a long way toward a better understanding of the problem.

Discussion

The topic for this chapter is not popular in or out of the church. When times are uncertain there is a natural tendency to pull inward, withdrawing from the pain of others. One thing that should be underlined in this chapter is that none of us is immune from the plight of economic dislocation. I certainly never planned to draw unemployment at any time during my working career. When conducting workshops for the unemployed in Denver I soon learned that unemployment is a "closet" problem in many churches. Those who are unemployed tend to hide this fact. They may be deliberately snubbed by others, even others in the church. There is a certain amount of stigma attached to the experience.

As I think back over the material shared in this chapter I feel that I may have presented a one-sided view of poverty. Living in sub-standard housing arrangements, for example, does involve a number of inconveniences and even added stress. On the other hand, in the most meager of circumstances there are positive features. The YMCA experience, for example, included the development of temporary community for me that would not have been the case if I had stayed in one of the better hotels in Hollywood. At the Y, I chatted with a young man from Nigeria and met a young woman from Canada. One of the desk clerks recognized me by name when I returned late at night after being on the street.

One important future possibility is to imagine a sharing of strengths and weaknesses across social class lines. Those who struggle through dark days of poverty can contribute new understandings to those who have never known economic reversal. Those in a comfortable situation likewise have things to share. Years ago while completing undergraduate work I interviewed a man who was staying at one of the missions in Seattle. This man took me on a walking tour of downtown Seattle. I was impressed by the way he saw small things I was inclined to overlook. He spoke with the imagination of an artist as he pointed out the sight of workmen on a new building project. He watched this building under construction every day and took note of all the subtle changes. He had a sense of pride in his community. In the midst of big plans and heavy concern maybe we all need the patience to look at the simple sights around us and to be more responsive to our own and others' joys and sorrows.

I have a personal dislike for the way much of the programming in the church is planned with only the middle-class in mind. A very popular international organization, for example, has dominated the field of Christian issues in relation to family life in recent years. Those who are given attention by this organization are generally people who have achieved considerable personal wealth. It is important to consider the kinds of conflicts that might surface in the family over such problems as whether the family should go to Vail or Aspen for a skiing vacation. But this kind of conflict means very little to a family where the real issue is who will get the single sandwich for lunch. Family relationships are going to be a bit more difficult when people awake in a cold house or apartment knowing that they will not have heat for weeks because there is no money to pay for a fuel delivery. The poor are under-represented in the formal life of the church. But they must not be ignored if the gospel is taken seriously.

Chapter 3
"Father, I Need a Drink"

The title of this chapter comes from a 1970 film about Seattle's Operation Nightwatch. In that film Rev. Bud Palmberg, founder of the program, is shown watching emergency medical personnel lift a body up into a waiting ambulance. As he reflects on this scene Bud remarks that this was a man who had promise and that maybe if someone had reached out to touch him with caring when he was a youngster he would not have ended up dead on the street from acute alcoholism at the age of 47. But the pain in those reflections is cut short by the awareness that others are out there and that they cry out for God's love. Sometimes the exchange with such a person begins with the plea "Father, I need a drink."

One of the immediate problems in discussing alcoholism in this book is that this may only perpetuate the myth that alcoholism is a problem for "street people" or for "Skid Road." This reinforces the denial behavior of the alcoholic who takes pride in pointing out that he/she is not an alcoholic because he/she is not a Skid Road derelict. Only about five percent of all alcoholics wander the downtown streets in the final stages of alcoholism. Alcoholism, one of the major health problems in America, cuts across all social class lines, all levels of employment, unemployment and most age levels.

Background

One of my first pastoral calls over 30 years ago was made in the home of a young housewife who attended the church periodically. This woman was regarded with pity by people in the church because her husband "had a drinking problem." I did not know what to say to her about alcohol abuse. I had no personal experience to speak from and no formal training

72

in alcoholism. The alcoholic husband worked regularly. He went on drinking binges every weekend. As I recall he had an interest in tropical fish and kept a large aquarium in the house. I talked with him on one occasion about fish but never talked directly with him or his wife about the disease of alcoholism. This is a good example of denial on two levels, that of the alcoholic and co-alcoholic and that of the minister.

At the same time I also made calls on an elderly couple living across the street from the parsonage. Their story is another example of how a pastor might become involved with alcoholism without being very effective. I share this story only as a point of departure to suggest how very different involvement with alcoholics is on the streets at night. The woman in this other family was very frail and seldom moved out of her chair. On every visit that I made I watched as her husband helped her drink a "hot toddy" heavily laced with alcohol. Her hands shook so much that she could not get the glass to her mouth without assistance. I went along with the husband's comment that she needed the drink because of many health problems. I never saw this woman as someone who was dying of alcoholism. She died several months after I first met her. I happened to be present near the time of her death and helped the local mortician carry her body out of the house. This was in a small town. The mortician ran a low-budget operation. He made such calls by himself. If I had not been around, the husband of the deceased would have been pressed into service to help carry the body of his wife out to the waiting hearse.

It is tempting at this point to launch into a lengthy discussion of definitions of alcoholism, how the body handles alcohol and other very important issues. Alcoholism is a major health problem in the country. Unfortunately it is now sometimes given less attention because of the sharp increase in interest in other drugs. Since it is something everyone needs more information about a separate chapter of more information is included in the last section of this book.

Personal Glimpses

As part of my preparation for ministry on the street I completed a course of study on alcoholism that included a field placement at a major detox facility. I followed regular counselors on their rounds and also interviewed some of the patients as part of the routine processing after admission. More than one hundred alcoholics are housed in this facility. I remember the stench of strong body odors as I walked into a room. It was the practice to pick people up in the street with a van and then to deliver them back to the same street in the same van after release. Unfortunately, this often meant that someone who was really hurting for a drink was dropped in front of a tavern. Sometimes people were re-admitted only hours after leaving the premises.

In this large detox facility I was impressed by the uniqueness of every "alcoholic." One of the most interesting situations for me was the occasion when two police officers came looking for a man. They identified one particular patient and then proceeded to interrogate him about a shoplifting episode. I watched this exchange. It became obvious to me that the man was in blackout at the time of the shoplifting. I was fairly sure that he had in fact taken the merchandise. But the whole experience was a mystery to him. He could not remember his behavior over a period of several days while he was in an alcohol-induced blackout, not an unusual experience for late-stage alcoholics.

On the streets at night alcoholics are also individuals, everyone with a special background and unique aspirations. It would be impossible to share all of the stories. Two men may serve as a brief introduction to some of the issues around alcoholism from the perspective of the street late at night. One night a middle-aged man appeared on the street in downtown Tacoma. He complained to me about sore feet and said that he was afraid he would go into seizures. Several days before our encounter he had started out from a city in Oregon, headed for the Expo in Vancouver, Canada. At that time he had $600 and was driving a car. He lost his car and most of his money during a drinking spree before crossing the border from Oregon into Washington. He did get as far as the Canadian border but he was in such an obvious state of disarray that the customs inspectors denied him admission. He turned around and started the trip back to Oregon, never seeing the Expo. I walked him to a detox facility, listened to his tales of woe and gave some immediate comfort/counsel.

Another alcoholic stands out in my memory because of his gentle appearance and sparkling eyes. At one time this 60-year-old was a very successful owner of several businesses. Two of his children were college professors. He died in the arms of a detox worker at a public detox facility. Two months before his death he chatted with me on the street. He opened the conversation by saying that he wanted to talk about peace. He said that he assumed I knew what he meant. This was his way to open the door for talk about God and life and death.

"My Name is Bill and I Am an Alcoholic"

Many of the encounters on the street are chance encounters for brief periods of time. There is seldom opportunity to really know the details of a person's life. To become more familiar with the alcoholic career that results in a person ending up on the city streets I interviewed a man known to the Seattle Operation Nightwatch ministry. This man, Bill, has introduced himself as an alcoholic at AA meetings for the past ten years. But he has been able to stay sober during only the last two years. Now he attends AA meetings every week.

Bill is in his late 50s but looks much older. He lives in a modest two room apartment a few blocks up from Seattle's downtown business district. Bill has many health problems. The most serious of these problems involves an abnormality in his heart and total circulatory system. He survives on a monthly SSI check. One of his pleasures is the opportunity to sing in the choir of a small downtown Lutheran Church. He is also a volunteer in the Operation Nightwatch office and for other agencies in the city. Bill has never known regular employment except for a period of three years in his early 20s when he was in the Army. He has been in and out of more jails and detox places than he can remember. He has spent more time "on the street' than in rented housing.

From the age of 19 to the age of 55 Bill's periods of sobriety came primarily as a result of involuntary withdrawal from alcohol because of incarceration. He served three different prison terms for periods varying from three to four years. Except for these years Bill recalls almost daily heavy use of alcohol. He had his first drink at the age of 17. For a period of about two years he stopped at only one or two drinks per drinking episode. He first became intoxicated at the age of 19. His drink of choice from the age of 19 to 21 was Southern Comfort Whiskey. At about the age of 21 he switched from whiskey to "anything with alcohol in it." This included wine, beer, whiskey and a variety of products such as sterno and rubbing alcohol. He recalls long periods of time when he drank constantly, day and night.

The experience of going into the service was the trigger for Bill's first drinking spree. He was discharged from the Army because of his drinking. Bill now says that drinking always made him feel "more confident," more "open" and more "relaxed." While drinking he could do things he would never be able to do without drink. This included having fun as well as breaking into stores and stealing.

For Bill the most extensive treatment came as part of his years in prison. In one prison he had easy access to a psychiatrist. This professional told Bill that he had a "pathological tendency to escape reality." The drinking was interpreted as one way to escape from the undesirable. From these encounters in prison Bill started to re-examine his relationships with people. Now he freely admits that he has problems in letting people get close to him. Although Bill has been through many detox experiences and the full range of downtown missions, he credits his present sobriety to his own thinking. For him keeping sober is "not easy." It is most difficult at night when he is alone and strong urges to drink come back.

Responses

Helping the Co-Alcoholic

Sometimes in street ministry the challenge is to work with the spouse or friend of an alcoholic. One night in St. Louis, for example, I met a middle-aged man in the Greyhound Bus Depot. He was alone and wanted to talk. His major concern was his wife's excessive drinking. She often became abusive when drunk. One of his coping strategies was to take long walks. I suggested that he get involved with Alanon. I was surprised when he said that he had never heard of the organization, an AA model for family and friends of alcoholics.

People in the immediate family tend to see the problem before the alcoholic. As a result, the spouse and children have a longer period of time to become sick themselves. Some professionals in the field consider the spouse as more in need of special help than the alcoholic. This does not mean that the spouse is neurotic, which in turn drives the other to drink. The alcoholic drinks, engages in alcoholic behavior and everyone in the family is affected in the process. It is the drinking that causes the sickness for all concerned. One of the first steps toward wholeness for the co-alcoholic (the spouse of the alcoholic) is acceptance of the fact that he/she is not "at fault" for causing the alcoholism.

The alcoholic's need for treatment may be obvious. Sometimes it is more difficult to see the hurt in other members of the immediate family. The alcoholic family, like all families, is a social system composed of individuals each with many ·

77

inter-related needs. Every member of the family has physical, psychosocial and spiritual needs. In the total experiences of individuals the judgments coming from important others are very important. We are social beings and respond quickly to feedback concerning self-worth. Sometimes we are in situations which encourage an open expression of feelings and experiences. Other times there are few opportunities for openness. Although past events have made major contributions to our feelings of self-worth, it is the present which must be given primary attention when trying to understand problems. How does one regard himself at the moment? What is his habitual pattern in relating to people who are close to him? How does he express negative and positive feelings? These simple questions are important for everyone.

It is easy to imagine how the alcoholism of one family member might influence other family members if we regard the family as a social system. Many therapists today approach the family from this perspective, drawing upon such traditional resources as the work of Virginia Satir (1964). People in a social system like the family relate to each other through processes of communication that are both verbal and non-verbal. The communication always involves the delivery of content as well as many other messages including critical messages regarding self-worth. Some messages are evasive. People struggle to read clues about themselves as they watch and listen to others in the family. In the alcoholic family communication processes are not working properly. Basic psychosocial needs are often frustrated.

In normal exchanges there is a reciprocal sharing of verbal and non-verbal clues during which all parties to the exchange participate freely. If a spouse is drunk or irritable because of extensive drinking the exchange is distorted. The co-alcoholic is placed in the awkward situation of being forced to focus on the alcoholism since it begins to dictate all family events while at the same time he/she is unable to get the normal self-evaluation from the alcoholic spouse. The co-alcoholic often falls into the dysfunctional pattern of looking at the alcoholic for signs of personal worth. If the alcoholic is not drinking on a given day, for example, the spouse may "allow" himself/herself to have a good day.

In the case of the co-alcoholic as well as the alcoholic it is imperative to understand that trauma and pain can flourish beneath a facade which is used to maintain some resemblance of control. The spouse often struggles in ways which only serve to increase his/her anxiety. Over-involvement in church work may be part of this struggle. The co-alcoholic can be very lonely while giving time to church projects. He/she may also do a lot of praying, trusting for a moral change in the alcoholic while giving no attention to the problem as a disease.

As conditions become increasingly desperate the spouse of the alcoholic is usually the first to experience some of the sensations of total loss. He/she begins to fear that the entire family is falling apart. He/she may feel a considerable loss of self-esteem when thinking about the loss of the affections of the spouse because of the first love for the bottle. His/her feelings for the alcoholic shift back and forth from sympathy to complete disgust. This amount of stress can contribute to any number of "stress diseases" including migraine headaches and gastro-intestinal disorders. The children in the family suffer in their own ways. They may need professional help to disentangle the conflicting messages coming from an alcoholic parent. They may also need assistance in working through dysfunctional adaptions which they have made to the situation. This includes, for example, the assumption of a "hero role" as a child to "redeem" the family in the eyes of the community.

Reality Confrontation

On the street, one of the most important contributions of the street minister is to be part of reality confrontation for the alcoholic. I will often pull an alcoholic back from endless talk about philosophical issues to help him/her focus on the real problem. One recent encounter will suggest how to re-focus in a more realistic way. In this particular situation the problem was heroin addiction but the pattern is generic for other forms of drug abuse including alcoholism.

Stan noticed my clergy collar as I approached him on a downtown street. He immediately started to talk about the evils of heroin. Seven years before our chance meeting he had lost two fingers in his right hand in an industrial accident. He held up the disfigured hand for me to see. After this accident he was given pain medication. As he told the story to me, he said that when he learned that he could get similar effects from heroin he switched to the illegal drug and has been shooting up ever since. He seemed to place considerable importance on the fact that a doctor had first turned him on to a drug as a way to relieve the pain after his accident. This suggested a picture of himself as the victim of circumstances. I listened as he went on to describe how he had become very adept with the needle. He often helped his buddies ''get on'' by finding veins and hitting them with the needle. Stan then expressed a lot of self-hatred as he said that his sister, a paraplegic, worked 40 hours a week. She dragged her paralyzed legs into a wheelchair and worked. He was just a ''junkie.'' That day he had stolen a $100 item from a store to get his day's supply of drugs.

The reality confrontation for Stan came as I responded to his story. One of my first approaches was to invite him to go back and re-think the story which he shared. I then repeated parts of the account, including the comment that he had been turned on by the doctor after his accident. I asked Stan to think about this in a different way, bringing in ways in which he took an active part in his own drug use. It was not someone else who shoved the needle into his arms. He did the job. He had a part in creating the problem and he would need to take bold steps to get out of the rut of being a heroin junkie. I was simply reinforcing the reality that Stan must take more responsibility for his own behavior. Based on experiences with others who cry out for help I know that the road to recovery is difficult. Considerable desire and motivation must come from the person who is addicted.

Few are in the position to confront a stranger on the street about his/her pattern of alcohol abuse. But many people are in a position to engage in reality confrontation with friends or family members. One way for an alcoholic to get into treatment is through the use of planned confrontation. Excellent teaching films are available on the process of confrontation at work and in the family. Wherever confrontation occurs there are basic steps which must be kept in mind. These steps are very straight-forward but they are not always easy to see through in the actual contact with an alcoholic. If one talks to the alcoholic in generalities he/she can very easily evade the issues. A spouse, for example, can complain that her husband never takes her out. The alcoholic husband can easily come up with times when he has, in fact, taken her out or he can give lists of reasons for not doing so. An employer can lecture about the need for "high morale." The alcoholic employee can talk all around this. Both come away from the exchange satisfied but the alcoholic keeps on drinking.

In an effective confrontation the people responding to the alcoholic are direct and specific. In the family confrontation is best done with the help of an alcoholism counselor. A small group of people well known to the alcoholic usually become involved in this confrontation. Prior to the confrontation the group plans how to handle the situation. An important part of this planning is the drawing up of a specific list of behaviors. A spouse, for example, can list the times he/she has been forced to wait hours on end for the wife/husband who never shows up. He/she may also specify the times when the spouse has been just too drunk to go to work. Older children may bring up how they felt when they brought a friend home only to face a drunken scene. If the specifics are sufficiently clear, the alcoholic will find it difficult to deny the problem. In the work setting the best advice for a supervisor is to focus upon actual work performance. This places the burden of diagnosis on the counselor where it belongs and it also introduces a level of specificity that cuts through the evasiveness of the alcoholic. In the confrontation at work the supervisor can either turn to formal records or start keeping such records if they are not currently available. These accounts should list days absent, poor workmanship, failure to attend meetings and other details of job performance. An ultimatium can then be given to the alcoholic that he/she is to get into a program of treatment or lose the job.

For those who work regularly with alcoholics it is necessary to turn again and again to the tactics used by the alcoholic to remain out of treatment and ways to respond to these tactics. There must be a keen alertness to the natural tendency to blame everything and everybody for problems. This tendency together with the strong pressure to postpone any decision until the next day can kill the alcoholic. In the family the alcoholic will blame his/her deterioration on the national economy, a nagging wife or husband and a long assortment of external things including the condition of organized religion. At work, alcoholics are very creative in finding scapegoats for their troubles. Subordinates are blamed, the condition of the machines or ''the competition'' or ''the flu'' are used over and over again as ways to cover up for irregular behavior because of constant drinking.

Taking People to Detox

One important response to the alcoholic by a street minister is to help people get to a detox facility. I have done this in different cities. The specifics of this process vary depending on the type of detox system in any given city. In Seattle, Denver and Portland, Oregon, for example, a van that is run by the city routinely picks up alcoholics to deliver them to a public detox facility. When I was in St. Louis there was no such service. Tacoma, Washington does not have a public detox van, neither does the Hollywood district of Los Angeles. If a city has a transportation system for alcoholics it is very unlikely that this sytem will be operating throughout the night. A minister on the downtown streets must therefore turn to other options when trying to help someone who is going through withdrawal or in danger of starting this process.

In Portland, Oregon, I often walked men from downtown across the Burnside Bridge to detox. One night I saw an older man on the street. He seemed to be in pain. I said something like "are you hurting, do you need help?" This led to the question "Do you need to go to detox?" When he responded in the affirmative I gave him partial support by holding him under one arm and walked beside him along a city street and out on to the Burnside Bridge. In the middle of the bridge this man stopped and took a bottle of cheap wine from an inside coat pocket. After taking a long drink from this bottle he shoved it down in the general direction of a pocket. But he missed the pocket and the bottle fell to the concrete, breaking into a hundred pieces. We continued across the bridge in a driving rain to the public detox place where my friend was admitted.

When I bring new volunteers into the program of late-night ministry I stress the importance of detox. In the ideal situation detoxification is the first step toward recovery. After going through detox the alcoholic then enters a treatment program and begins the long process of recovery. But unfortunately, most middle and late stage alcoholics who use a public detox facility do not go on to recovery. It becomes only one of many detours down the painful road which ends in death. In such circumstances detox becomes part of the humanitarian reaction to the alcoholic. Being in detox removes the street alcoholic from the danger of physical abuse from others and provides an important monitoring during temporary withdrawal from alcohol.

The possible life-threatening complications during withdrawal recommend professional intervention. It is difficult to outline specific withdrawal reactions since the pattern can vary somewhat from individual to individual. Two distinctive withdrawal syndromes have been identified however, "minor withdrawal'' and "major withdrawal." The minor withdrawal occurs normally within the first three days after the last drink has been taken. Major withdrawal is experienced primarily by late-stage alcoholics. It occurs from three to five days after the last drink has been taken. One of the problems of the public detox facility is to monitor symptoms with sufficient accuracy to prevent the early release of a patient who may be in danger of going into the more dangerous major withdrawal symptoms. With public assistance patients there is always pressure to limit the number of days of detox care.

In the best of circumstances there is a regular monitoring of physical changes during withdrawal by a nurse or someone with medical training. If life signs indicate a threatening condition for the person immediate medical intervention can be applied. Specific body reactions within the basic body systems are monitored. In minor withdrawal the most commonly seen problems of the circulatory system include; rapid and irregular heart beat, higher pulse rate and increases in blood pressure. During minor withdrawal there is a hyperactivation of the central nervous system. One possibility is uncontrolled muscular contractions or seizures. These seizures can be dangerous and sometimes are fatal. One of the recommended responses to these episodes is to protect the person from hurting himself. In general the seizures during minor withdrawal are very short in duration. A detox facility routinely administers Dilantin to anyone with a history of seizures. On occasion other drugs may be used. Other problems associated with minor withdrawal include hallucinations, insomnia and gastro-intestinal disturbances producing vomiting, diarrhea and/or nausea.

In most cases minor withdrawal is completed in about 48 hours. An obvious turn-around in symptoms can come abruptly. A small percentage of alcoholics (about five percent), however, reach a danger point when they start getting better. Instead of moving on through withdrawal they go into a major withdrawal pattern. The "DTs", or delirium tremens, occur in major withdrawal. This is a very serious condition. When the alcoholic goes through the DTs without medical help the mortality rate can be fairly high. In the DT experience the person becomes totally disoriented. He/she may need to be restrained from possible damage to self.

Some degree of hallucination is typical of minor withdrawal. But in major withdrawal the hallucinations and tremors of the DTs are much more intense. The patient becomes confused and frightened. He sees things like bugs, snakes and rats, sometimes blown all out of proportion in terms of size. If he hears voices these voices may be threatening him. Additional symptoms of major withdrawal include heart fibrillation, a life-threatening condition. The prevention of major withdrawal is one of the major reasons for medical attention during withdrawal. Administration of appropriate drugs including the cautious use of minor tranquilizers is part of the medical treatment. These drugs are used with care because they can set up a secondary dependence pattern in the alcoholic.

Encourage Participation in AA

Another reaction from the street minister is to encourage alcoholics to attend AA meetings. Sometimes I will repeat and then reinforce the first three steps of AA, reaffirming the need for personal surrender, belief in God and the turning of life over to God. Alcoholics Anonymous is the most successful recovery program for alcoholics. A stockbroker (Bill W.) and a surgeon (Dr. Bob) started AA in 1935 as they struggled to maintain their own sobriety.

The bold-self-searching and powerful personal affirmations in AA provide the kind of high-level motivation essential for sobriety. These are reinforced by the social support in AA. In AA recovering alcoholics meet as a group. Something happens when people get together which is somewhat similar to the synergistic effect of mixing different drugs in the body.

A result occurs which is far in excess of what could have been accomplished by the elements acting individually.

One of the major agenda items in an AA meeting is the personal testimony of life as an alcoholic. People stand in front of others and give minute details of a wide range of honorable and dishonorable behaviors. There is an atmosphere of total acceptance of the person. AA members hug each other and tell each other how much they are appreciated. It is this kind of fellowship which fosters high loyalty. In recent years some AA clubs have found that they must handle the problem of increasing numbers of non-alcoholics coming to meetings simply because they want to belong. Sometimes the AA meeting is the most enthusiastic and warm meeting in the neighborhood. Alcoholics take the final greeting in a meeting, "keep coming back," seriously.

People with a background which has included serious involvement with the church may have problems relating to the AA format. In some meetings members are very free in their use of four letter words, for example. Although the program is spiritual in nature it does not promote specific organized religious creeds. Members are advised not to use meetings as a stage for recruitment to a specific church. When a person with a strong church background allows himself/herself to participate on the level of shared experiences and emotions the AA connection can be a very powerful force for both sobriety and positive living in general. I know many people who are active in both the church and AA. Some of these people seem more enthusiastic about what is happening to them spiritually in AA than they are about what is going on in the church.

The 12 Steps of AA

1. We admitted that we were powerless over alcohol — that our lives had become unmanageable.

2. Came to believe that a Power greater than ourselves could restore us to sanity.

3. Made a decision to turn our will and our lives over to the care of God as we understood him.

4. Made a searching and fearless moral inventory of ourselves.

5. Admitted to God, to ourselves and to another human being the exact nature of our wrongs.

6. Were entirely ready to have God remove all these defects of character.

7. Humbly asked Him to remove our shortcomings.

8. Made a list of all persons we had harmed, and became willing to make amends to them all.

9. Made direct amends to such people wherever possible, except when to do so would injure them or others.

10. Continued to take personal inventory and when we were wrong promptly admitted it.

11. Sought through prayer and meditation to improve our conscious contact with God as we understood him, praying only for knowledge of His will for us and the power to carry that out.

12. Having had a spiritual awakening as the result of these steps, we tried to carry this message to alcoholics, and to practice these principles in all our affairs.

Spiritual Ministry

At different points in this chapter, reference has been made to the spiritual dimension in responding to the alcoholic. Alcoholics cry out for sincere involvement by ministers. I do not know anyone who has recovered without going through a spiritual conversion. God is taken very seriously by people when they are in the middle of desperate circumstances surrounding chemical dependency of any kind. This bold frontier for ministry is too often sadly neglected by the church in general.

As an illustration of the very powerful and personal experiences of some alcoholics during recovery I was impressed by the sharing of a friend in St. Louis as she talked about her life before becoming a volunteer in a helping agency. She talked in some detail about her experiences in going through an alcohol treatment program. One day she was having a very difficult time. That night as she was lying in bed she suddenly became aware of a presence at the foot of the bed. She was overcome by this presence and by either the impression of words or actual spoken words to the effect that "everything would be all right" and that she would have "peace." For her this was and is regarded as a direct meeting with the Divine.

One of the most powerful books for church leaders who are interested in alcoholism is the 1966 publication of John Keller titled "Ministering to Alcoholics." The first chapter of this book and Keller's personal witness on pages 63-66 should be required reading for any pastor who wants to help alcoholics and their families. He gives a good argument for more involvement by the clergy, refuting the idea that alcoholics should be responded to only by specialists and the attitude that alcoholics do not want to see a minister. The minister may, in fact, be a primary source of help at particular stages in the process toward recovery.

One of the most important contributions of Keller is that he discusses at some length the theological basis for work with the alcoholic. As Keller suggests, we are made to be human which includes the acknowledgement of our imperfections. We are meant to love, trust and obey God for everything. We get things out of perspective when we place ourselves in the center. We think that we should be perfect when we can't be. We place ourselves at the center when God should be there. Since we can't be perfect we feel guilty before God.

One of the generic problems of man is to fully accept the reality that God loves him as he is. In Christ God comes among us and shows us that he really loves us and wants us now and forever. He is not against us. We need to be and have been reconciled unto Him. "We are his redeemed, justified, and forgiven children." Christ gives us the courage to accept ourselves as accepted in spite of being unacceptable. The ultimate relationship in life is a relationship with God in Christ. "We are persuaded that nothing and no one can separate us from Him and His love."

One can anticipate how Keller relates the Christian experience to the problems of the alcoholic. One of the major areas of need for the alcoholic is a basic relationship with God. Many recovered alcoholics talk about a "walk with God," or about "spirituality." They reach the point where they feel that God really loves them. The second major area of change for the recovering alcoholic involves changes with respect to estrangement from self and others. Alcoholics often express feelings of not **really** being loved and not **really** being accepted by others.

One of the common adjustments to feelings of low self-esteem is to over-compensate by trying to be perfect. The alcoholic may make vain efforts to be superior and perfect, like God. This generally results in little inner peace and keen disappointment in the lack of perfection in others. Through alcohol the alcoholic "unconsciously learns to evade the gnawing, vague anxiety of his unresolved estrangement" (Keller, 1966, p: 12). But the alcohol backfires and becomes his master.

To work effectively with alcoholics it is imperative for Christians to take a close look at their own spiritual health. One of our problems, according to Keller, is that we are inclined to come to God as we think we ought to be, not as we really are. We have problems in letting God be God. We often hold back from trusting him with all our heart. When we acknowledge our own needs we are better able to walk with the alcoholic instead of standing above him in a moralistic or judgmental position. "We see that the alcoholic is not someone unlike ourselves but our brother in sinfulness and need. He is one of us. Our relationship with him ceases to be marred by moralism." (Keller, 1966, p. 13)

Keller is critical of the Christian community when this community operates on distorted images of who a Christian is and what a Christian is like. He suggests that Christians sometimes wear masks and pretend. He also points to the problem of getting caught up in "sins" instead of **the** sin of estrangement from God and self. Another difficulty is that the Christian is sometimes made to feel that he must always be "strong in the Lord." This does not allow for the normal admission of weakness. We are called upon to be honest in expressing what is instead of always talking about what ought to be. Honesty is desperately needed in the area of love. We are often told that love should never hurt when in actuality there are times when true love does hurt. As Keller sees the church we must be "the fellowship of the imperfect, of the sinners, before we can be the fellowship of the redeemed."

> *The crucial question for us as estranged persons, persons who cannot be who we were created to be, is whether or not we have a meaningful, personal redemptive relationship with Christ as Lord and Saviour, and whether or not we are able to live in meaningful personal relationship with ourselves and others, particularly with members of our own family. (Keller, 1966, p. 22)*

In his publication, Keller outlines basic approaches for counseling alcoholics. He reinforces the need to see these people not as alcoholics but as individuals with names like Mary, Jane and Bob. He calls for an outreach based on shared needs on the part of both the alcoholic and the counselor. The alcoholic does not need moralizing, lecturing or someone to pamper him or overprotect him. The alcoholic does need someone who understands alcoholism and who understands how he feels and cares about him and his feelings.

Discussion

Although alcoholism is a major problem with many implications for the church there are few formal discussions of the topic within the church. I have also discovered that alcoholism counseling is seldom included as part of seminary training for clergy. The idea that alcoholism is a disease is repugnant to some people. Sometimes this is interpreted to mean that the individual has no role in his/her recovery. That, of course, runs counter to the knowledge that strong efforts are needed on the part of the alcoholic before recovery can proceed. For others the disease concept contradicts teachings in the church which equate alcoholism with sin. The alcoholic would be the first to admit estrangement from God. But other aspects of the problem also need attention. At some stages in treatment, in fact, it would be life threatening to ignore such realities as physical needs while concentrating only on the spiritual.

There is a growing body of information on the details of such topics as how the body processes ingested alcohol. One of the most promising fields of research is the study of genetic factors which predispose a person toward alcoholism. It remains disappointing, however, to see considerable disparity between academic knowledge and intervention with alcoholics. Late stage alcoholics on the city streets in particular have benefited little from the expanding knowledge about alcoholism.

Before the 1970s it was customary for the police to routinely round up the Skid Road winos, herding them into a drunk tank at the city jail. This practice was changed with new definitions calling public inebriation a symptom of a disease, not a form of criminal behavior. A public detox facility is the modern equivalent of the revolving door drunk tank. In some cities, however, public inebriates still represent a disproportionate number of police arrests. They are very vulnerable to arrest because of their total lifestyle which puts them in conflict with most of the downtown population.

A lengthy book could be written on the respnse of the church to alcoholism, especially on the city streets. Years ago one popular form of home mission activity included regular attempts to hold street corner services aimed at the winos. In most large cities today there is a remnant of this form of activity. I see my work in street ministry as one of the new directions for downtown outreach. As I have suggested repeatedly in this book, I do not preach on street corners. I become involved with people on a one-to-one basis. I try to see the alcoholic as a person. I appreciate the honesty I see in most situations. Sharing pain and hope at a deep level with alcoholics is one of the very special experiences of street ministry.

Chapter 4
Powder, Pills and Needles

"Drugs" often become so embroiled in political heat that it is very, very hard to take a balanced look at the problem. The data that some sources give can seem alarming. We are told, for example, that as many as 5,000 Americans try cocaine for the first time every day. About five million people are believed to be using this one illegal drug at least once a month. James Lieber (1986) reports that one private psychiatric hospital in Syracuse, New York seldom admitted cocaine abusers during the 1970s but that during the 1980s 40 percent of the hospital's beds were set aside for this use.

In the midst of the considerable talk about drugs there are few who become actively involved in efforts to redeem addicts. Street ministers are one of only a small band of professionals who actually walk the turf with addicts who are using drugs or who have recently used drugs. Face-to-face contact with these "outlaws," modern-day lepers, gives fresh insight into the problem.

Background

Unfortunately, the abusive use of drugs is too often placed in the category of strange behavior by people who haunt the city streets in search of their next fix and/or customer. Drugs of one kind or another are used and abused by many people in a variety of ways in our society. Research indicates, for example, that between 10 percent and 23 percent of all workers in America use dangerous drugs on the job. One of the most alarming aspects of on-the-job use is its prevalence in high security, technical defense/space related industries. This form of drug abuse poses a much greater potential threat to our society than the use of drugs by people who live on a meager hand-to-mouth level on the city streets. But it is the abuser on the streets who gets most of the attention.

Some drugs we now label as illegal have been used in one form or another for years. The entire range of behaviors involved in the use of opium, for example, are highlighted in the stories of Sherlock Holmes and in other literary works. Going back much farther in time, coca leaves, the base for cocaine, have been consumed by Peruvian Indians for nearly 5,000 years. The chewing of this leaf produces mild stimulation and serves to suppress the appetite. Modern problems with cocaine use were precipitated by the scientific discovery of how to extract the cocaine alkaloid from the coca leaf in 1860.

Amphetamines were used widely in the 1930s as stimulants. When law enforcement agencies closed down amphetamine laboratories this opened the door for new stimulants including cocaine. Cocaine became the most popular recreational drug starting in the late 1960s. Cocaine use in the 1960s and 1970s involved the snorting of very expensive cocaine. In the 1980s the method of administration changed from snorting to either smoking freebase or shooting up, both much faster routes to the brain. At the same time, the cost of cocaine dropped dramatically. This resulted in a considerable increase in the number of serious drug addicts.

Drug abuse has devastating personal and social consequences. But the actual practice of taking an illegal drug can, at least momentarily, produce effects which may be regarded as very pleasasnt. In 1805 a 20-year-old English youth by the name of Thomas De Quincey purchased a popular anal-gesic for a toothache and started his lifelong use of opium. His response to his first dose as recorded in his book "Confessions of an English Opium-Eater" points to an immediate sensory experience that helps to explain drug use in general:

> . . . I took it: and in an hour, O heavens! What a revulsion! what a resurrection from its lowest depths, of the inner spirit! what an apocalypse of the world within

me! That my pains had vanished was now a trifle in my eyes; this negative effect was swallowed up in the immensity of those positive effects which had opened up before me, in the abyss of divine enjoyment thus suddenly revealed. Here was a panacea . . . for all human woes; here was the secret of happiness, about which philosophers had disputed for so many ages at once discovered; happiness might now be bought for a penny, and carried in the waist-coat-pocket; portable ecstacies might be had corked up in a pint-bottle; and peace of mind could be sent down by the mail.
(De Quincey, 1907, p. 179)

One contemporary report of the perceived positive effects of drugs is included in a newspaper interview with the Rev. Nelson "Ned" Graham, son of the evangelist Billy Graham. This interview by Steve Maynard appears in the Tacoma, Washington Morning News Tribune for February 26, 1989. Ned Graham, the youngest son of Billy Graham, was serving as an Associate Pastor of a Baptist Church at the time of the interview. He reflected back on his days as a student at a church-related University in the Puget Sound area. From the age of 19 to 26 he used drugs and alcohol. He did not take drugs as a way to rebel. As he explains it, "I enjoyed drugs and alcohol. I was sort of infatuated with it."

One of the most difficult combinations of factors to understand and manage in the treatment of the drug addict are those factors involved in social relationships. Many years ago the noted sociologist Howard Becker called attention to the social side of marijuana use. He referred, for example, to the ways in which the experience of smoking marijuana is defined and re-defined by peer pressure. As he reported then, a basic amount of social learning is necessary to achieve the addictive effects of the smoking. There is considerable literature about how individuals respond to drugs as individuals. But more information is needed on the very important social dimension.

In my work on the streets of the city I am often confronted with the ways in which social interaction patterns serve to sustain drug abuse. The legal response to addicts stigmatizes them, pushing them further into a counter-culture of drug use. I have seen people on the street the day after their release from jail. They generally go immediately to old haunts and old friends, often only a few blocks from the jail. They do not know people in parts of town where drugs are seldom used. I am also told that a serious addict can get a feeling comparable to direct drug use simply by being present to watch someone else shoot up. This is a strong form of social influence. Among addicts there is also the practice of using the needle on a friend to help him/her "get it on."

One of the more frightening aspects of contemporary drug abuse is the escalation of violence around the behavior. It has become commonplace to hear reports of drug-related homicides. The chief of police in one city said that a few years ago drug transactions were fairly relaxed exchanges. If an addict promised to pay on Saturday this was often taken to mean Sunday or Monday. But with the increased involvement of gangs the ground rules have changed. Now a Saturday payment date means Saturday. If there is no payment the person who owes money is likely to become the target for planned shooting. First warning shots are fired at the knee-cap. If this does not produce the desired effect increasingly more life-threatening shots are fired. Violence is one aspect of drug addiction that captures considerable interest in the media. Less attention is given to other equally important aspects of addiction.

Personal Glimpses

Personal glimpses drawn from first-hand contact on the streets at night can be misleading since they disproportionately represent only the more serious, late-stage addict. The life style of these people should not be taken as representative of the total pattern of addiction. For example, people often ask me how drug addicts are able to buy their drugs. I reply that the three most common ways to get money are prostitution, becoming part of the sales force and/or petty theft. But in reality these are not the biggest sources of funds for drugs. Most drug abuse is done within the context of normal work and family roles. All too often money which should go for food, clothing, vacations, retirement and other basics is instead used to support a drug habit. With continued use an addict may end up on the streets. Not all of the people on the street are late-stage addicts, however. Another problem in sharing material like that which follows is that the street scene is in constant flux. The amount of drug activity reported on the streets of one city below has changed dramatically over the time for the writing and editing of these pages. The direction has most recently been toward a marked reduction in the highly visible drug transactions. Careful study is needed to determine if this is representative of a reduction in actual drug use or just a geographical redistribution of the problem.

For a period of time I often witnessed open drug dealing on the streets of Tacoma at night. Since I wear the clergy collar, I was seldom propositioned personally. When dressed more casually on one occasion, however, stepping out onto the sidewalk from my parked car was like walking onto a used car lot. I was told that "he has the stuff" and someone else called out to inform me that he had a better deal. One night a woman came up to me on a downtown sidewalk. I did not know her. But she had talked to one of the regular volunteers months before. At the time of this chance meeting she was back on the streets after a time of going straight. Now she was on drugs again. She held a cigarette in one hand and her next fix of cocaine in the other hand. After we talked I hugged her as part of my expression of concern and caring, a rather peculiar situation for a minister to be in. When drugs are heavily used street ministry is in the middle of the active drug scene. This presence offers a great opportunity to become a meaningful part of dramatic change in people.

All in A Night's Work

As indicated above, it is hard to keep up with the changing face of the drug scene. As this is written in final form, Tacoma no longer has the group activity on main streets. When this activity is on the night turf covered by a program of ministry it is imperative to reach out in many ways to those who are addicted. To illustrate possible kinds of involvement I want to share contacts over a two-hour period one night several months ago.

My first contact this night was with a young man whom I had seen on and off for about a year. Jim was a professional musician at one time. While working he never made less than $50,000 a year. But now he walks in the shadow of a heavy drug addiction problem. This night be expressed guilt at being found on the streets again and told me that he really was making progress in getting his life together. He also said that he was bothered because, as he saw it, I had always been there for him, had always given to him but he had not given in return.

Shortly after this exchange with Jim, another young man, Stan, wanted to talk on the sidewalk. I initiated this exchange by asking him how he was doing. This was my first contact with Stan. I told his story in the last chapter when discussing the need for "reality confrontation" in the case of any form of drug addiction including alcoholism. As I reported in that context, Stan first started using heroin after experience with a prescribed pain medication. This night he was very remorseful about his whole life and really wanted to talk. He described drug addiction as a "no win" situaton. He admitted to walking out of a store earlier in the day with a $100 item which he then sold to buy his drugs for the day.

A few feet from Stan on the same downtown sidewalk a young woman wanted to talk. We first met through a third person who was a drug dealer. Tonight this woman said that she needed and wanted drug treatment. She was addicted to heroin. I explained one option which demanded a $75 entry fee and offered to cover this fee for her. Another woman standing near us immediately spoke up requesting referral to the same facility. Both of these women were given cards for follow-up the next day.

Inside a tavern a few minutes later I ran into the young woman who was first introduced in this book as a cocaine addict. This night she was very glad to see me. She said that her boyfriend had just been released from jail. We talked about how she might get it together to keep an appointment leading to in-patient treatment. This encounter was very short but did serve to maintain continuity with her.

Out on the sidewalk again I met the middle-aged man who was first introduced in Chapter 1 as "Ray" under the subheading of "I Don't Know How to Do a Funeral." In that brief narrative I mentioned that I had not seen this man in a year. He did return after extradition from another state. This night he reached out a hand in greeting. He said that he was now "getting it together" but his companions and presence on the drug strip would suggest otherwise. A few weeks before this encounter I had gone to visit Ray at his request during his recovery from a brutal knife attack. He said that he had "died five times" on the way to the hospital and in the hospital. Now he seemed to be recovering in spite of the loss of some lung capacity from the wound. When he said that it was about time for him to talk about his soul I encouraged this. But I told him that he would have to change to get to God. He would need to approach God in a different way than he handled his other relationships. This meant, for example, that he could no longer be the con operator he was now. He would need to surrender, to become a different person than he was. His response to this was to put an arm around my shoulder and walk with me across the intersection. I interpreted this response to mean that he was not yet ready for a serious spiritual journey.

All of the above encounters came during a short round of the downtown streets one night. They suggest the kind of exchanges that a street minister will get into as part of the process of reaching out to people who are active on the drug scene.

Next I introduce a few more specific people I have seen many times.

"Where's the Reverend?"

This question was shouted down the empty hall of a hospital as a young woman alternately slumped to the floor and staggered forward toward an exit She was going through withdrawal from a long run of cocaine use. I was "the Reverend." I walked beside her, an arm around her shoulder, assuring her of my presence and guiding her back to the emergency room. This was a small episode in a long night/day for me as I tried to help this young woman.

That night my first contact with her came when I saw a person all alone in the middle of a downtown sidewalk late at night. I could not tell from a·distance if it was a man or a woman. As I approached I saw that it was Jill, a woman I had first met two years before. This night she was in deep pain. I happened to be on duty with a new volunteer recruit. I immediately put an arm around her and told her that I could not stand to see her suffer like this. I said that I would take her to detox and get her started in a treatment program. With the help of the new recruit for ministry I walked her to the car.

As we drove through the streets of downtown Tacoma I felt the personal agony of watching a friend writhe in the physical misery of a body out of control. She nodded off to sleep. Then she awoke with a start, arms thrust out. Unaware of where she was. But conscious of my presence.

My first goal was to get her to the emergency room of a local hospital which has a large alcohol/drug treatment program. I knew that I could not take her to the small public detox facility because they are only able to manage people going through withdrawal from alcohol. With considerable effort I was able to help Jill struggle into the emergency room. A medical technician on duty informed me that there was no public detox facility anywhere in the city or county or anyplace in Seattle/King County immediately available at that time of night. In desperation I asked if the hospital could keep my friend over night while I worked on a plan for treatment. After a professional huddle the staff told me that they could offer three days of detox for $1,500! This made me mad. The service was completely out of the cost range of both my friend and my program of ministry.

In the parking lot Jill said that she wanted to go home. She thought that she could just walk a block or two, not aware that she was now in a different part of the city. I told her that I was not ready to give up. I wanted to try another hospital. We drove across town and walked into another emergency room. This time I was told that they might be able to admit her if she had some problem in addition to drug withdrawal. Hoping that they would find a broken bone or something else of medical interest, I suggested that they examine her.

It was in this hospital that my friend wandered off down the hall looking for an exit and crying out for me. When I got her back to the E.R. area with the help of a security guard she nodded off in a deep sleep. The physician on duty said that she might sleep for as long as six hours. It was now 1:30 a.m. I told the staff to watch her and to call me when she awoke. Then I made my way home. I found it hard to sleep as I lay in bed, thinking of my friend and the hopelessness of the case. I tossed in bed, occasionally drying tears with the bed sheet.

At 6:00 a.m. I was paged to return to the hospital. Jill was just waking up. I helped her stand and walked her to the car. Now my plan was to get her some breakfast and then to follow the recommended steps to get her into treatment. When I showed her the menu at a fast-food restaurant she pointed to a $3.95 breakfast special and asked if that was too much money. I told her that she should order what she wanted. Although she had not eaten in three days she only poked at her food, putting most of it in a doggy bag to take along when we left the restaurant.

Over breakfast my friend talked about her feelings when she saw women working as waitresses. She said that she was overcome with a sense of envy. She wanted so much to have a regular job. We talked about a vocational training school and the kind of work she might be able to do. She said that she really wanted to get her son back and most of all wanted to be free of drugs.

After breakfast I drove to the local office of the Department of Social and Health Services (DSHS). This office would open at 8:00 a.m. We were the first two people to enter the building when the doors opened. This was a necessary visit because it was the first step in getting financial support for treatment through a fairly new program, the State's Alcohol and Drug Addiction Treatment and Support Act (ADATSA). With approval from DSHS the interview process could begin at ADATSA in another building across town.

I walked up to the intake window at DSHS with my friend. She was given a stack of forms to complete. She tried her best to stay awake for this chore but kept nodding off. I took over the task, asking her questions, completing the forms and telling her where to sign. This was a difficult task but we did complete the work. I assumed that we were now on the way to treatment. But this proved to be a very naive assessment of the situation. Back at the intake interview window the worker on duty looked at the forms and complained that some of the boxes were not filled in. These corrections were made. Then we were told that the system was over-taxed and that we would need to come back in a week for the actual interview. At this point I knew that I had lost the battle. A person actively addicted to cocaine was told to go back out on the street to encounter regular offers for drugs while waiting for an intake interview!

When I said goodbye to my friend that morning I cried. She did have her appointment card for the interview which was set for one week into the long future. That seemed like an eternity away at the time. I drove back to DSHS on the day of the interview but she did not show up. Several nights later I saw her on the street. She was strung out on drugs, very agitated, striking out at buildings and people and expressing feelings of deep guilt about failing to keep the appointment. I also saw her getting out of a car late at night in another part of town which made me anxious that she might be turning tricks to buy drugs.

One might wonder how I could develop such strong feelings for this person. There have been times when she has run across the street to greet me with a hug and a kiss. I have been present when she has been depressed and ashamed of her appearance, and at times when she has been very neat in appearance. She often greets me with words like "Rev. Dean" or "Father" and "it's so good to see you." During my time of contacts with Jill she asked me to visit her father in the hospital. He had serious circulatory problems which necessitated the amputation of one leg. I called on him in the hospital. The other leg was also amputated. I visited with him in his home when he was released from the hospital. These and many other contacts pulled me into a pattern of sincere caring and concern for Jill. As I write this, my prayer is that I will be able to complete the work of spiritual and physical transformation which Jill cries out for in her own way.

A $900 Daily Heroin Habit

At 6:00 a.m. in the darkness of an October morning I drove through the deserted streets of an Eastern Washington City. A married couple were in the car with me. This was to be the temporary end of a journey which began at 1:30 a.m. in Tacoma. Since no pubic detox was readily available in Western Washington I decided to escort this couple to Eastern Washington where a drug treatment center was holding two beds for me. Before I share the final exchanges that morning I want to go back in time to re-trace some of the highlights of this series of encounters around heroin and cocaine addiction.

I first met Sandra while looking for someone to help me learn Spanish. A mutual friend introduced her to me as a person fluent in both English and Spanish. Months later she told me that she had, in fact, run into me on the street a year earlier. That time there was no conversation and I had no memory of the meeting. She remembers the night as the time when one of her friends shot and killed another friend. She was in shock on the street when she turned and saw me, a stranger, wearing the clergy collar. She wanted to talk but was afraid to. Later that night she went to the apartment of the fellow who had pulled the fatal trigger. He was lying on top of the blankets in his bed, the pistol on his stomach, crying his eyes out. Sandra tried to comfort him.

That traumatic shooting event months ago was not the most immediate pain for Sandra when we were formally introduced. She was concerned about her husband. He had been picked up by the police on a charge of possession of drugs and was in jail. I offered to visit him. This ordeal of visiting lasted for some 40 days. It was always difficult because her husband, Richardo, spoke almost no English. On my first visit I noticed that his hands were marked by skin sores from the use of needles. During the jail time he appeared for our talks with white medication on the sores. The sores healed up. He seemed to improve physically in other ways over the weeks. But he fell into periods of deep depression when he became aware of how hard it was for me to keep in touch with his wife. She was on the street and in a Skid Road Hotel. Sometimes I could find her and at other times I did not know where she was.

While Richardo was in jail he was escorted into court for a hearing. I attended this hearing with his wife. An interpreter was available. The defense attorney assigned by the court was bi-lingual. But the judge did not understand Spanish. It was interesting to observe his actions and to hear him talk about Richardo. During his verbal dialogue about the case he defined the young man as "someone with a third grade education." The man's wife later told me how hostile she felt at that time. It appeared to her and also to me that the judge was making a hasty evaluation based upon his own inability to understand the language. Richardo was, in fact, fairly well educated. He could read very well. But he could not speak or read English. The judge also expressed the conviction that he would never pay any fines and the only way to get anything out of him was to keep him in jail. His sentence was set, based on the fact that he had a prior offense on the books. It turned out that this information was false since Richardo was working at the time of the alleged former offense. His name happens to be a very common Mexican name.

As I have indicated, during Richardo's jail time I kept in touch with his wife on the street. She said that she was on heroin. I shared her deep feelings about her husband including extreme anxiety about his welfare. She seemed willing to do almost anything to raise money to get him out of jail. And she talked about her own drug problem. When I pressured her about going into treatment she said that she had some legal things to take care of and that she needed to raise money for her husband.

There were times when she appeared haggard and thread bare. At other times there seemed to be a little hope. One night she asked me to take her to McDonald's for some food. She had money. She ordered and paid for a large amount of Chicken McNuggets for herself and a cup of hot chocolate for me. I had learned that such a display of money meant only one thing, that she was again into drug dealing. A few weeks after the McDonald's visit Sandra told me that she had reached the point where she was shooting up a gram of heroin at a time and going through something like $900 a day in the process of maintaing her habit. She deliberately selected drug dealing as the way to raise this money. As she explained to me, there were other things which she could do to get the money but she felt that selling drugs was "the least damaging to others!"

Two days before her husband was released from jail, Sandra was picked up by the police. It took me four days to find her in jail because she had used a different name when picked up. On my first visit with Sandra in jail she was in the middle of withdrawal. She was very sick. She sat across from me in the interview room, arms covered with bruises and scars. She was barefooted. She shook all over. During the next visit she was over most of the chilling but had moved into a period of deep depression. She expressed strong doubt that she would ever see her husband again. She just knew that she would be taken to prison again. As she informed me, she had done some three years in prison and "could not stand going back." According to her they "burned her out" when she was in there before. As she saw things her only out was to end it all. She talked of suicide. Another pain which pushed her in this direction was the knowledge that her mother was dying or near death and that she had not, could not see her. During this visit with Sandra I took off my black suit coat and placed it around her shoulders when I saw that she was cold and shaking from the cold. I talked openly with her about the suicide issue. I attempted to set up a contract with her that she would not do anything until I had the chance to see her again in three days.

Two days after this jail visit Sandra was transported to a city some 200 miles away. This other city had a warrant out for her over an unpaid fine of some $350. Given her condition the last time I saw her I felt obligated to visit her in the new jail. I found her husband on the street, invited him to make the trip with me and we drove four hours to see her. We arrived only minutes before the visiting time was over. She was very happy to see her husband. We were told that she would be going to court that very night. She felt that she would be released on the spot because her husband had some $175 and she had $40 or a total of about half of the money needed. Her husband and I waited around in the small town for the late-night court session.

As it turned out she was brought into court as the only woman with eight other inmates. They were led into the court in lock-step, hand-cuffed with a strong rope strung between each pair of hands. She later confided to me that this was a very dehumanizing experience. When she was called to stand before the judge Sandra did very poorly. She appeared very

106

bitter and challenged the judge about her fine and days in jail. The judge took a very negative approach to the case, insisting that Sandra remain in jail to do the 15 days as sentenced. Sandra was crushed at these words. We watched as she was led back to jail. After this scene we drove through the night, getting back to Tacoma at 3:30 a.m. the next day.

After that long night I lost track of Richardo on the downtown streets. Five days later I got a call from Sandra in Seattle. She had been able to talk friends or family members into paying the total fine and giving her bus fare out of town as far as Seattle. I drove up and gave her a ride the rest of the way back to Tacoma. At first I tried to locate a temporary place for her to stay. It seemed impossible to find her husband. She was determined at that time to get off heroin. We asked around on the street and a friend of hers told us her husband was staying in one of the old hotels in town. I went with her to that place. She stayed in the hotel lobby while I went up to his room. In my limited Spanish I told him that "a friend" was down in the lobby and that this friend wanted to see him. (This was the way she wanted me to announce her presence.) He dressed quickly and followed me down the steps of the hotel. I watched as they embraced and walked out of the hotel lobby arm in arm, together again after two months of separation.

A week passed before I heard from Sandra again. She finally invited me out to dinner. She and her husband were staying in a cheap motel near the downtown drug strip. I drove them to a Chinese restaurant and they paid for an expensive family-style dinner. Back in the motel room I became aware that Sandra did not have basic items of clothing when two friends of hers came by the room to give her and Richardo some clothes. The irrational spending of money is one of the characteristics of addiction.

When Sandra stepped outside to talk with friends Richardo went into the bathroom. After his trip to the bathroom his behavior changed. He locked the door and pulled a chair up under the doorknob. Then he pulled the window shades closed and yanked a metal covering off a heat vent so that he could stare at the exposed wires. When Sandra returned to the room her first question was whether or not he had been to the bathroom. When I told her that he had she immediately cussed him out for "shooting up" while a "priest" was around. During this heated exchange I noticed the point of a needle, part of the "works" (hypodermic syringe) sticking out of his back pocket.

Sandra was thrown into a fit of despair, crying as she said that she just could not stay with him through the night when he was acting like this. She said that he had an ounce of cocaine in the room and that he would just keep shooting up until it killed him. During these tense minutes Richardo expressed a desire to talk with me. Sandra interpreted for him as he spoke in Spanish. He said that he wanted help in getting off drugs and then added that his wife was also "sick."

I called a detox facility located some 180 miles away in Eastern Washington. As I have indicated, no such facility was available at that time in Western Washington. I told the facility to hold two beds and offered this as an option to the couple. Sandra served as my interpreter in discussing this with Richardo. After some delay they agreed to go with me. Her words at the time implied that she was at the end of her rope.

It was now 1:30 a.m. I had been going all day. But they loaded up their few personal effects and we started off on a four hour drive through the darkness over a mountain pass to Eastern Washington. There was opportunity for a lot of talk during this trip. At one point Sandra said that she was very thankful for what I had done for both of them but that she just did not understand why I was doing it. In one city along the route we stopped at a 24-hour restaurant. Sandra went into the rest room. I became anxious when it seemed like she would never come out. When she finally returned to the car she said that she had done something that was "very hard to do." Then she asked me if I had any idea what it was like to flush $800 worth of drugs down the toilet.

At 6:00 a.m. we parked in front of the drug treatment place. There was an emotional parting. I was tired after driving through the night. Sandra said that she would not be able to make it without God's help. We talked about a total surrender of life, giving all to the Lord. I prayed with her, tears in my eyes. They gathered up three plastic bags of personal effects and I walked with them into the facility where I left them after a final round of hugs. I drove back to Tacoma, watching the early morning light signal the dawn of a new day. I wish that I could say that this was a successful ending but it was not. Sandra and Richardo walked away from the treatment facility and became involved again in drugs. At the time of this writing he is again in jail and I am working with her through the formal system of getting into another treatment place.

Responses

Many people have been or will be in the situation where they must respond to a problem of drug abuse. Individuals, families and organizations including schools, churches and places of work struggle over how best to respond. I see the importance of both hope and tough love. In the church in particular it is sometimes difficult to set limits but this must be done. In street ministry, responses to drug problems include those which are summarized below. General strategies within these responses have implications far beyond work on the downtown streets at night.

Helping Family Members

"The Crips Have My Wife"

On Hollywood Boulevard in Los Angeles I often ran into Bill, a middle-aged man with graying beard and faded blue jeans who was the leader of a motorcyle gang devoted to Christian witness. One of his main interests was the distribution of a hand-out sheet which proclaimed the virtues of a Godly life. I was impressed by Bill's sincere desire to help others on the Boulevard. One night as we chatted he shared a personal problem with me.

Bill said that he had married a young woman a couple of years before our meeting. But the woman was not living with him at the time. The Crips, an L.A. street gang, were beginning to move into some of the abandoned buildings in the Hollywood area. Bill's wife had been taken in by a leader of this gang. She was given drugs and according to Bill kept in an empty house against her will. After hours of investigation Bill located the house and called the police. He stood outside as the house was raided. When his wife came out the front door Bill was thrown into a state of shock. He told me that her total appearance had changed. The heavy doses of many different kinds of drugs had a devastating impact upon her physical appearance and personality. She did not want to talk to Bill.

Although my response to this sad story seems very simple it merits consideration. I listened to Bill. Listening is a powerful way to help. Unfortunately all of us are caught in situations where others dominate the scene by talking on and on about some grand scheme. We need lessons on how to listen to deep pain. That night I listened. After listening I did something else which is also seldom done in the narthex of a church. Bill is a tough looking, bearded man who rides a motorcycle. He is not the kind of guy one would identify with sentimentality. But after first telling him what I felt like doing and getting his go-ahead sign I moved closer to him and hugged him. Others caught up in personal tragedy because of the destruction of loved ones through drugs need the personal assurance that someone does care deeply about how they feel. Bill cried that night. I walked with him through part of his misery.

"I Can't Face Him Alone"

This plea came from a woman who is a leader in her church. She told me that her son was "on drugs." He had been sleeping in his car for several months. When he called wanting to see her she called me, asking if I would go with her for the contact. She explained that she had not been feeling well and just did not feel up to the contact. I agreed to make the 10-mile drive with her to the location designated for the meeting.

When we stopped to let her middle-aged son in the car he seemed glad to see her. He also seemed very up-tight and nervous. She drove to a local restaurant where we ordered food which she paid for. At the table her son expressed his anger that she would bring me, a stranger, along when it had been two months since he had seen her. Then I knew the other reason for my presence. He wanted to see her because he needed money. She felt that my presence would make it more difficult for him to get money from her. His specific plea was for $200 to pay for one month's rent. His mother said that she had given him money in the past and that it had never really helped. I was caught in the middle of this argument.

This became a very difficult situation for me. With my experience in working with people on drugs this mother hoped that I could "talk to her son." As it turned out he was not ready for this kind of talk. He wanted money and was bitter because she refused to immediately give him a check. He started to attack her verbally. She is a retired person and can not respond to every request even when she wants to. She told me that she is still paying the remainder of a $5,000 bill which he ran up while completing a drug treatment program in the past. She forced treatment at that time. It did not turn him around. He walked out of the program before it was completed. On our drive away from the restaurant after the lunch I sat in the front seat of the car. The mother was driving. Her son was in the back seat, directly behind me. I was afraid that he might attack both of us. When I got out of the car to let him out of the back seat he slammed the door shut behind me

111

and continued to hassle with his mother. She then opened the door on her side of the car and got out to stand beside the road. At that point her son got out and stalked away. He threatened to kill himself, telling her that she would never see him again.

This woman was so distraught by the experience that I offered to drive her home. She said that she had gone through some fainting spells recently. The stress was just too much for her. I was very sorry for her but appreciated the opportunity to experience a little of the difficult feelings which family members must live with in trying to both love and respond objectively to loved ones who are addicted to drugs.

A Mother With Cancer and A Daughter on Drugs

Another example of how complicated things can get is illustrated by 40-year-old Jane, a mother I have seen often on the streets at night. I consider this woman a friend. We first met when she was working as a bartender in a downtown tavern which caters to blue-collar and street clientele. I saw Jane as a hard-working woman, holding down two jobs to pay her bills. In addition to tending bar she did house-cleaning in a downtown hotel. A few months after our first meeting this woman was diagnosed as having cancer. When she went to the hospital I visited her. In her difficult condition while in the hospital she was more concerned about her daughter than about herself. While she was getting intensive treatment her daughter was running out of control on drugs.

I offered to talk with the daughter but this never became possible. Mostly I simply listened and gave emotional support to Jane. After the hospitalization there were long weeks of struggle to come up with money for rent and food. When Jane did have money her daughter would steal from her. A TV set, stereo and other items were taken from the house and sold by the daughter to get drugs. One time Jane removed her wedding ring before taking a shower. While she was in the shower her daughter took the ring to a downtown pawn shop. Jane has been trying to come up with the money to reclaim this valuable ring. There were other crisis events in this family including the frightening experience of a murder just outside the front door of their low-income residence. Drugs can play havoc in the daily life of people who at best struggle with problems of bare survival.

Responding to Crisis Needs Including Transportation to Detox

Facilities

In street ministry volunteers and regular staff must be aware of the crisis medical needs of drug addicts. One night on Hollywood Boulevard two young men came running up to me. They said that a friend was sitting on the sidewalk a few blocks away in "bad shape" after taking drugs. I hurried with them to the friend and then they both left the scene. The young man in crisis was sitting up on a backpack, head in his hands. When he looked up at me I saw both the fresh glow of a recent suntan and the look of pain in his eyes. In response to specific questions he said that he had taken rock cocaine and crystal a few hours earlier. At first the reaction was pleasant. This euphoria did not last long. It was followed by frightening spells of first feeling cold and then feeling very hot with spinning sensations in his head. He had used drugs before but these sensations were new and very unpleasant. He seemed honestly frightened. I called 911 and waited with him until the paramedics arrived.

The personal scenarios in this chapter may leave the impression that very few people actually make it through detox and treatment. I have seen recovery begin and the results of years of drug-free living. During the month when this chapter was written the Tacoma program of Operation Nightwatch helped to place four people in a program for heroin detox and treatment. At that time a fee of $75 was charged to begin this process. Some designated contributions made the placements possible. As I indicate in my reports of late-night encounters the process of getting people into treatment is difficult because of the lack of services for the medically indigent.

In the discussion of detox for alcoholics there was some mention of the problems around withdrawal. In the case of drugs other than alcohol it is also true that the periods during which drugs are not taken, withdrawal, are the most difficult times for the addict. Withdrawal for the alcoholic can be life-threatening. In the case of cocaine and heroin withdrawal the problems are more psychological than physical. But they can be very, very confusing and painful for the addict.

After a run of cocaine use it is not unusual for an addict to fall into a spell of prolonged sleeping. Another part of the withdrawal pattern related to cocaine use is profound depression. This can be a time of major crisis. There may be talk of suicide. Depression can set the stage for getting into treatment if used appropriately by people in touch with the addict. Withdrawal from heroin is associated with flu-like symptoms. The heroin addict may say that he/she was so sick that death seemed like a release from the pain. The biggest worry may be that they will live to continue the torment instead of simply dying and ending it all. I have seen the uncontrolled body shaking, pained facial expressions and inability to sit through an interview while going through heroin withdrawal. It is not a pretty sight.

An Advocate With the Criminal Justice System

Contacts with some part of the Criminal Justice System are not unique to programs of street ministry. If one is involved with a family member or friend who is into drugs he will very likely confront this system. Unlike alcoholism, there is considerable ambiguity regarding the appropriate community response to drug addiction. Much of the criminal justice system is devoted to the arrest and incarceration of addicts and

114

pushers, primarily those who are highly visible on the streets or working out of popular "crack houses."

The streets at night are seldom the place for direct exchange with any part of the Criminal Justice System. On the sidewalks and in taverns I seldom see police officers. They appear only to make targeted arrests or in response to an emergency call. They are also around as part of undercover operations. I tell people that they must get out of those parts of the city where there is heavy drug trafficking if they are really serious about getting off drugs. I reinforce this because staying in these parts of the city can only lead to both more drug use and doing time in jail. Unfortunately, jail is not a place to recover from drug addiction. In Tacoma and other cities the jail is a place for punishment, not rehabilitation. The limited medical help which is available is not oriented toward withdrawal problems in spite of the fact that 90 percent of those in jail are confined in relation to drug use. A "crisis cell" area is set aside in the jail for medical problems including the acute physical problems during withdrawal. But jail inmates are reluctant to request this special housing because it places them in a kind of solitary confinement, a very undesirable condition.

One important role for the minister is to be in touch with an addict before and during incarceration. The court hearing is time consuming but it is a very important experience for the individual addict. Any contact after the hearing will take on more significance if the minister has taken the time to sit with the addict in the courtroom. It is inappropriate for the minister to give legal advice. Sometimes the addict can be given suggestions about the merits of local attorneys who have experience with drug cases. After viewing the courtroom drama I also see the need to remind the people I see in jail that their behavior in court is important. I have watched as drug addicts have been so belligerent during a hearing that the judge is strongly inclined to issue the strongest sentence possible. The court likes to hear a repentant attitude and realistic plans for dealing with the addiction as well as plans for getting on with the business of work and family obligations.

115

Jail visitation can be a very important part of the total work of a pastor whether or not he/she is involved in street ministry. The clergy person has a unique advantage in having ready access to the jail. As a professional he/she can visit throughout the week in most jails in contrast to the very limited visitation rights of friends and/or family members. The clergy person is often given an interview room where the inmate can be seen in much more normal surroundings than the glass-enclosed areas which are part of the visit for most jail visitors.

In the jail visit it is important to follow the formal rules set by the jail. Absolutely no items can be given to the inmate, for example. I find it best to relate to the individual inmate in terms of his/her felt needs instead of bringing in a pre-arranged agenda to the visit. If the inmate is getting no other visits then I try to make fairly regular contact. When I leave I mention when I will return for another visit. Often it is important to serve as a liaison with family and friends on the outside. The jail experience is also often a time when the addict wants to talk about getting off drugs and also about his/her spiritual life. The simple presence of a clergy person in the jail to visit a specific inmate has many potentially positive results for the inmate. For one thing, this makes that inmate someone who is a little special in the eyes of the jail staff.

Spiritual Counseling

As in the case of alcoholics, spiritual ministry is a critical part of recovering for the drug addict. The world of addiction should not be dismissed by the church as a domain to be claimed by law enforcement and/or those with professional training in chemical dependency. On the personal level, addicts have frequent opportunity to turn toward the Divine in their daily battle with physical craving, hope and a sense of personal worth. The language may be different but the quest for the spiritual strength remains strong. A drug addict, for example, made a request when he saw my clergy collar. He asked me to "shoot a prayer upstairs" for him. Shooting up was something he was very familiar with. I am sure that in his own way he was familiar with an assortment of pleas and bargaining directed toward God.

One part of spiritual ministry is that a well-planned and honestly motivated religious service can have a powerful impact although no direct reference is made to drugs. I have talked with people who have spent time in jail and who tell me that they turned their life around as the result of a traditional church service conducted in jail. The hymns, prayers and sermon were not given from the perspective of the addicted person specifically. But they did speak of estrangement from God, forgiveness and Divine love. The transforming power of God's grace can work miracles. No special background in drugs is needed to plan or participate in this form of outreach.

My work is primarily on a one-to-one basis. On the individual level one approach is to encourage again the basic steps of AA. The drug addict can be encouraged to attend NA (Narcotics Anonymous). The steps are the same as in AA. There is power for change in the honest personal affirmation of failure, the presence of the Divine and a turning of life over to God.

Peer support for the drug addict may be more of a problem than is true for the alcoholic because those addicted to drugs are always close to illegal behavior. This demands a very strong break with many former friends with whom powder, pills and/or needles have been shared. Providing support networks can be another aspect of the total outreach of the church.

In or out of jail one problem for any minister in contact with addicts is that it is all too easy for him/her to be pulled into the role of a doormat for the addict. When seeing someone in the confines of a jail it is natural to be sympathetic. Being in jail is not a happy experience. The inmate often says that he/she "did not do it." When a minister automatically goes along with such an account this may only make it more difficult for the inmate to face the situation realistically. Sometimes people are jailed inappropriately for something they had no

117

part in but as a general rule police do not arrest someone unless there is a reasonable basis for confinement as the law is stated. It is wrong to assume that someone is in jail because of "the system" with no personal responsibility. This is another place where reality confrontation is needed. In one situation which I beame involved in a young man was being held on some very serious charges. He also had a history of prior offenses. But he insisted in his total innocence. I could see no indications that he wanted to take any responsibility for his own behavior. Another person was also seeing this man in jail. This other member of the clergy seemd to totally embrace the man's view of why he was in jail. One of his contributions during an interview was to tell the inmate that the Apostle Paul had also been in jail! I failed to see any resemblance to this man and the Biblical saint. Ministers are not doormats. They are potentially powerful bridges to Divine grace. But such grace is predicated on honesty and a surrender of self. Prematurely pressing a blessing upon everyone can only make it more difficult to follow the necessary steps for personal transformation.

Another side of spiritual ministry which I have only recently come to appreciate with specific reference to the drug scene is that ministry must become much more bi-lingual and inter-cultural. As one way to more effectively serve the full range of people on the night scene I have recently attempted to learn a limited amount of Spanish and Korean. I find that this becomes much more than learning a language. There are many cultural differences that impact the way a minister is viewed and how the process of ministry is conducted. For the person from Mexico, for example, the priest is regarded very differently than he would be from the view of many people in this country. As someone familiar with the Latino culture and the life of the streets in this country informed me, someone wearing a clergy collar and walking among Spanish speaking people has a very powerful potential influence.

Discussion

It would be hard not to have strong reactions to the content of this chapter. One of the real dangers in any discussion of drugs is that the problems can be described in a way which only serves to make the problems more difficult. One of my real concerns is that people have a tendency to panic when it comes to drugs. They have images of a son, daughter or close friend going skiing in Aspen, being given drugs in the restroom of some night club and coming away hooked for life on cocaine or heroin. Some parents are horrified at the thought that their children will be turned on to drugs while playing on the school grounds. Most people do not use illegal drugs. In most social circles there are strong informal norms against the use of illegal drugs. It would probably make more sense to panic over the possible abuse of alcohol.

Recently I attended a workshop on organizational development. I expected a series of lectures on such specifics as how to write letters to foundations and how to make telephone calls to possible donors. Instead I heard a lot about the basics of how to build a solid organization including such general information as the appropriate role of board members in a non-profit organization. One of the best ways to combat drug abuse is to make sure that the basic building blocks of life are strong. It is important to know such specifics as where to go for drug treatment. But it is even more important to know how to build a total life. Family interaction patterns, education, times for worship, times for recreation and play plus meaningful work with adequate pay are all high priorities in the battle against drugs.

There is no frontier for ministry more challenging and with more potential for impact than work with drug addicts. Addicts know all about pain, social stigma, death and hopelessness. They experience heavy doses of guilt and remorse. Often these people have considerable talent. Most are young. They cry out for involvement by the church in ways which generate wholeness. This is not the time to add more layers of guilt.

It is a time to reinforce the value of every person within the Divine plan.

Another aspect of ministry to both alcoholics and drug addicts is that there is always a heavy sense of urgency. I am thinking, for example, of a 25-year-old woman I saw in a city jail. Her mother, a cocktail waitress, asked me to make the contact. Mother and daughter were not on the best of terms. The mother knew that her daughter was into drugs and felt helpless to avoid what she described as an inevitable tragic end.

The jail visit was one of my most positive of such visits. After I explained to the small 25-year-old who I was, she immediately spoke freely about her problems including her inability to talk to her mother about drug use. She did not see herself as a "drug addict" but did admit to casual use of drugs. She laughed and talked about her plans after her release from jail a few days after my visit. At the end of my jail visit with her I hugged her and wished her well. One week after her release from jail this young woman with dreams for the future was the victim of a drive-by shooting. She was shot on the sidewalk only two blocks away from the place where her mother worked. Death came minutes after she was rushed by ambulance to the Emergency Room of a near-by hospital. The chapter on alcoholism began with the story of the death of a 47-year-old alcoholic. This chapter ends with the story of the death of a 25-year-old who used drugs. One of the sad trends on the city streets is that death now comes much earlier for people who are crushed by chemical dependency. On the positive side as I re-read these pages before publication I can report remarkable changes over time for some people mentioned in this chapter. Now one of the "hard core" addicts sends me letters telling me that she is praying for me. She is now off drugs. Another recovering addict is a drug counselor.

Chapter 5
When the Night Has Been Too Long

My first contact with a suicide in process came while I was a volunteer for the Crisis Line in Seattle. Contrary to popular belief, a 24-hour Crisis Line usually gets few actual suicide calls. Most callers have other problems such as temporary depression or how to find emergency shelter. My first suicide call came from a woman who said that she was holding a razor blade to her throat as she talked. I followed the recommended routine of asking her to put the blade down so that we could talk and keeping her on the line until the call could be traced. I remember her words of shock when she looked out the window to see a police officer coming toward her house as I spoke with her.

Downtown ministry of any kind at night or during the day will inevitably become involved in suicide situations. Although the topic is seldom discussed openly except at the time of an actual suicide it is something that every helping profession must be ready to respond to. Hopefully the comments in this chapter will help place the behavior in perspective. This may be helpful on a personal level for anyne who has experienced a suicide in the family or for one of those now at high risk for suicide.

Background

The Extent of the Problem

Suicide is one of the most traumatic experiences for family and close friends to go through. It does not take a large number of such experiences for a community to realize that suicide is

121

a major problem. In the United States approximately 12 people in 100,000 commit suicide. This translates into some 25,000 such untimely deaths every year. In addition from 50,000 to 200,000 people attempt suicide. Suicidologists estimate that there are 200,000 to 400,000 people at high risk for becoming suicide victims in the United States.

In recent years there has been a growing interest in youth suicide. Suicide for young people reached a low in 1955 and then increased to 1977 when there was a leveling off of the increase. According to 1982 data the rate of suicide per 100,000 white males in the United States between the ages of 15 and 19 was 15. For the 20-24 age category at the same time the rate was almost double at 28 per 100,000. In terms of actual numbers of suicides nationally, in 1982 for the 15 to 24 age category there were 5,400 suicides. During the same time 202 suicides were reported for the 10 to 14 age category and only 40 for the 0 to 9 age category. Unfortunately, accurate statistics on black suicides were not maintained before 1960. The available data suggest that the suicide rate for black males is one half to two thirds that of white males of a similar age.

Males commit suicide at a rate which is three to four times the rate for females. Females, on the other hand, attempt suicide three times more often than males. Those females who do commit suicide are more likely to use guns than any other method with an over-dose of pills as the second most popular method. For males the use of guns is the preferred method with hanging as the second most often used method.

Old age is often discussed as a time in life when suicide risk increases. There is a significant difference between the sexes when considering older age and suicide. Males who are 65 and older have a higher rate of suicide at 38 per 100,000. For females in this same age category the rate is only two per 100,000.

The statistics on suicide reinforce the importance of everyone giving some consideration to the topic. None of us is far removed from the possibility that someone we know will threaten or commit suicide. Every minister must give some consideration to professional encounters in which the trauma of suicide is the main agenda. There is always the possibility that a crisis will develop when it is not possible to pass this crisis on to someone with considerable experience. The best referral may take time to arrange. Suicide situations call for immediate response. Downtown street ministers are more likely than any other ministers to encounter suicide behavior because such programs serve a high proportion of people at critical risk for suicide including homeless alcoholics.

The material on suicide in the second part of this book under "Additional Information" is some of the most important information in this publication. These pages cover such issues as: explanations of suicide, basic theories of suicide, crisis intervention in general and legal issues around the behavior. Following the pattern of other chapters, I will now go directly into some of my own personal encounters where suicide or the danger of suicide was the major presenting problem.

Personal Glimpses

"I Have a Loaded .38 Pistol"

I first introduced this encounter in Chapter 1 when talking about a selected number of downtown "lepers." As I reported in that chapter, a native American pulled me aside one night in a tavern on South Broadway in Denver. As I look back on that encounter I am reminded again of how different a direct contact is from the experience of talking with someone over the phone at a place like a Crisis Clinic. The tavern was dark. The man was a stranger to me.

When he talked about suicide and also informed me that he had a loaded .38 on his person at the time I was not sure what to do. In this and other situations it is not easy to act on the "best" response for a minister. I was not and am not a mental health profesional. Some kind of action was called for. I attempted to put the man in touch with his most recent professional contact, the local VA hospital. I must admit that I was relieved when some of his buddies came along and he drifted away from me. I would not have taken him to a facility in my car knowing that he had a gun.

Stopping Suicide in Process

The first experience with suicide in the late-night ministry of Seattle's Operation Nightwatch involved the program's founder, Rev. Bud Palmberg. He was called to the scene as a young man edged out of a hotel room window threatening to jump. Bud made his way up to this man's room and talked to him through the open window. When the man said that by jumping to the ground he could get his sister to listen to him Bud convinced him that in all likelihood the sister would never know about his death. A few minutes after this tense conversation began the stranger crawled back into his room.

When Bud felt comfortable with the emotional state of the man he went down to the hotel coffee shop for a cup of coffee. Before he could finish the coffee a hotel employee came rushing up to him. The young man who had talked of suicide was reported to have locked the door of his room with new shouts of "ending it all." Bud hurried back to the room. The hotel manager unlocked the door. Inside Bud found the man sprawled out on the floor, blood smeared over his body. He was trying to cut one of his wrists. Bub shoved the knife out of his grasp and used his tie as a bandage/tourniquet to stop the flow of blood before calling 911.

This young man did survive the suicide attempt. Bud visited him in the hospital. When he was released, Bud invited him to stay with a family in the church. Things seemed to be going along fairly smoothly. But when this family went on vacation the man set the house on fire. Bud and the members of his congregation did not immediately give up on the stranger. He was next invited to sleep in the church. One morning Bud was greeted by shouts through the locked door of his office. The man had locked himself in the room and cut his wrists. He then collected the blood in a paper cup and threw this fresh blood at the books which lined the office. After this episode the young man was admitted for treatment. He never returned to Bud's neighborhood. When last heard from he was in prison on charges of arson.

For me there is a personal sadness in repeating this story. Years ago while teaching a class in a community college I used the story as an illustration of suicide behavior. As I described the scene in the hotel room a young man in my class asked me not to be so graphic with the details. A woman in the class shared some of her own problems around the chronic health problems of her mother. I tried to be helpful regarding the parent but did not really talk with her about her own anxieties. Several months after the end of that school quarter I learned that this young woman who had completed my class took her own life in suicide. This makes me very aware of the need to take the topic seriously.

A Death Poem

As reported earlier, Seattle's Operation Nightwatch program once offered a few notel rooms to the homeless on a first come, first served basis. People who used these rooms could not find a place in the other emergency shelters in the city of Seattle. Sometimes there was no opportunity to follow-up on the very difficult problems facing folks who used these rooms. It was only after the fact that Rev. Norm Riggins became aware of the trauma a 17-year-old girl was going through. When one room was being prepared for a new guest the following few lines were found written on a scrap piece of paper. They reflect the deep hopelessness of the young temporary occupant:

To my friends I say goodbye
Hoping they won't ask why.

The pain is now too hard to take
So I've chosen not to wake.
Life is hell, you can't win
Giving up can't be a sin.
Now my so-called friends do not weep.
For my strength I no longer keep.
I can't bear to think ahead
Oh, how I wish I were dead.

A 13-Year-Old Boy Sees Nothing to Live For

A few years ago Father Don Erickson started a special street ministry to reach the children on Seattle's streets. I talked with Father Don early in this process when he was having a real problem getting any kind of financial support for his efforts. I bought him a piece of pie and a cup of coffee as we talked. At one point Don was in tears as he tried to share how he felt about wanting to help the "throw away kids" and not getting the support to do it. Back then I had no personal experience with the reality that street ministry does not automatically attract financial support. Now I have been through the difficult times and can better understand his feelings.

I wanted to know more about the work of special ministry to the kids on the street. Father Don talked about his experiences. One of the most difficult encounters he recalled came around the suicide attempts of Stan, a 13-year-old. Stan was a regular on the streets. He had been in so many foster homes that he had lost count. On the street he fell into a pattern of drugs, hustling people for money and petty theft.

There were two serious suicide attempts by Stan. Each time this 13-year-old took a large quantity of pills. Stan was wanted by the police. Father Don talked about his dilemma as he sat one night with Stan in a car parked outside King County Hospital. The boy was in pain. Father Don knew that a lot of pills were involved. He felt that medical attention was needed but also knew that Stan would be turned over to the police as soon as he was admitted to the hospital.

As Father Don recalled the long hours with Stan he mentioned how hard it was for him to watch a 13-year-old boy who was out of his mind from drugs and who talked only about wanting to die. As part of this death trip Stan sat for hours staring off into space while listening to the song "The Rose."

In this song as sung by Bette Midler in the Mark Rydell film "The Rose" strong symbols of life and death are highlighted. The song tells of a heart that is afraid of breaking, about the fear of waking and refusing to take chances.

Perhaps the most direct reference to self-destruction is the comment about the soul that is afraid of dying. This type of person is described as never learning to live.

The images of this song could be interpreted to mean that death is good, that it leads to better things like the seed dying in the winter to become a lovely rose in the spring.

Both the words and the compelling melody could capture the imagination of a teen-ager as in the case of Stan.

Stan did survive the two attempts at suicide. He was placed in detention at the Juvenile Center in Seattle. Father Don maintained contact with him. On one visit to the facility, Stan said that he wanted a new pair of tennis shoes. Father Don was able to get the shoes for him. Stan explained that he had walked lots of places where he was ashamed to be. Now he wanted to start out with new shoes, walking only where Jesus would be glad to see him.

"My Wife Will Never Take Me Back"

This was another encounter that I shared in Chapter 1. The man was sitting by himself in a booth near the door of a restaurant-cocktail lounge that I often entered late at night. I was drawn by his obvious manifestation of depression. The encounter is a good example of the possibility when being alert to others. Sometimes it is necessary to be "on the turf" with others and also to be sensitive to covert as well as overt messages. I was getting the strong message of depression and so I stopped to initiate a conversation. The man had been wandering the city streets for two days, afraid to return home. One of his spoken options was suicide.

One of the positive outcomes from this chance encounter was that I had the opportunity to see an immediate change in this man. I talked him through his pain and drove him home for a reunion with his wife. I followed up on this situation and had the opportunity to talk wth him after he had returned to work. He was urged to continue his involvement in a local congregation. Community supports were available. When we first met late at night he urgently needed someone to respond to his time of crisis. This is a time of keen opportunity for ministry.

Funeral for a 15-Year-Old

In street ministry there are few opportunities to participate in the formal ceremonies of the church such as funerals and weddings. But over the years I have had occasion to serve by helping at these times. One of the most difficult of these experiences was a funeral for a 15-year-old boy who had committed suicide. This boy was in a juvenile detention facility when he rigged up a makeshift harness and hung himself. He was a native American Indian from a family which had many problems.

I did not know this youth personally. I was asked to conduct the memorial service because of my position as the director of a late-night program of street ministry. There was standing room only in the funeral home on the day of the service. I tried to comfort the grieving mother, other family members and friends. The service seemed very awkward for me. At one point I invited those present to simply share something of their own feelings/experiences with the deceased. A few people did stand to speak out. Some expressed appreciation for my references to the strength of the Indian legacy and tradition. One of the strongest points of reference during the service was the reading of Psalm 23.

Reactions

This chapter has already included a number of possible reactions to suicide behavior. Following the outline of other chapters this section will mention a few of the responses which are more specific to late-night street ministry. These responses should serve to reinforce important basic strategies in the management of suicide situations in general:

Helping the Survivors of Suicide

In late-night ministry there are opportunities to talk with the survivors in places like hospital emergency rooms and/or in taverns, cocktail lounges and night spots. While working in St. Louis, for example, I decided to spend some time in an affluent cocktail lounge near the airport one night. I ordered a Coke at the bar. Before I finished this soft drink a man sitting a few bar stools from me moved closer and ordered another Coke for me. Then he shared his experiences. He was a commercial pilot with one of the major airlines. He was in St. Louis for only the one day. The trip was made so that he could attend the funeral of a buddy who had committed suicide. At one point he asked me if I knew what it was like to sit through a closed casket service with a room full of strangers. One of his major concerns was that his young daughter find happiness and hope and a true reason for living.

It is helpful to know some of the standard reactions which close family members/friends have after a suicide. It is not unusual for the survivors to have physical symptoms as part of the stress reaction. This may include feelings of being physically drained, having severe headaches and not being able to sleep or rest.

Often there is a tendency to feel deep guilt as the events surrounding the suicide are recalled over and over. Survivors talk about regret over what they should have done. Sometimes the suicide message is taken as being intended directly for them personally. One sign of growing out of the deep guilt is the ability to let the person who has committed suicide be responsible for his/her own behavior. Survivors need to know that the state of mind of the suicide person is such that it blocks out all others. There is a total preoccupation with personal, internal states. Others including family and friends are just not taken in. The person comes to see only pain and has fears about death. There is very little concern about what others are thinking and/or doing. Survivors were cut off by the suicide person and therefore should not feel the crushing guilt which too often rises up to smother those who are left with vivid memories of the person and sometimes the minute details of the day of the death.

Most communities have good resources for talking through the trauma of suicide. One way to get in touch with these resources is to call the local Crisis Line or Crisis Clinic. Survivors talk about personal embarrassment and shame. The suicide is described as one of the most traumatic events possible, something which changes "all of life." It can be regarded as the ultimate rejection. Survivors are put at high risk for attempting suicide themselves. For some, this is the time to think about things like the deceased "needing" them. Many survivors identify with death. They may come to see it as a solution to their own problems. It is a time to take a hard look at personal coping skills. Survivors may get into a form of restricted thinking similar to that which characterizes a suicidal person. They need encouragement to widen their options, to see that death is not a good solution and that pain is only temporary.

Survivors must allow themselves to still express love for the one who has committed suicide. It is okay to talk about the victim. All thoughts can not be simply shut off because it was a suicide. This is the time to re-affirm the value of the spiritual. Faith in God is critical. Those survivors who move positively through the experience talk about a process of growth in which they see life differently. They realize more fully than ever before that material things are not the most important part of life. People and relationships are given added significance. They become more sensitive to others, realizing that what we say and do can affect another's self-esteem.

Putting People In Contact With Others

At different points in this chapter there has been reference to the need for contacts with others. This is another way the street minister can be helpful. One of the most important contributions I made in the situation involving the depressed man who had not been home in two days was to put him back in touch with his wife. Suicidologists recommend giving people telephone numbers to call in an emergency. When the person who is at high risk is seeing a counselor this counselor will generally keep a record of family members to assist in the process of strengthening contacts when this becomes necessary. In the high-risk populations such as the elderly social isolation is one of the most dangerous precursors of suicide.

131

Using Community Net-Works

In a recent case involving a pastor and a suicide victim which was given considerable attention by the mass media the family of the deceased sued the pastor and his church for not making routine referrals when the victim expressed strong suicide tendencies during counseling. The major problem during this counseling was that the pastor interpreted the suicide in spiritual terms only. He used a restricted field of vision when trying to help a person with major problems in the restriction of vision. The court ruled in favor of the pastor and his church.

In ministry we must strive for a professional management of serious problems. There should never be a time when anyone who is serving as a minister tries to keep someone from getting specialized professional advice within a specific area of need. There are several kinds of community resources which can form a supportive network for a person at risk for suicide. The Crisis Line or Crisis Clinic number must be given and written down. Sometimes a community will have agencies which provide services for specific populations such as youth who are at high risk. Community mental health centers often include emergency crisis outreach teams as well as walk-in crisis counseling which the person at risk must be made aware of. At another level, there should be some focus on basic life skills including the building of better coping skills and assertiveness.

The Spiritual Dimension

No part of the suicide scenario is devoid of spiritual considerations. There is great power for the person at risk and for survivors in a very serious touching of the Divine. People cry out for hope. The gospel is a message of hope and unconditional love. As in the case of chemical dependency, the faith of the one who ministers is most crucial. One who regularly spends time in meditation, tapping deep resources of God's presence for daily living, and who places proper emphasis on the practical demands of life can be a strong fortress for others who walk near the edge of a great gulf as they fight recurring cycles of pain, fear, guilt and depression.

In this chapter mention has been made of some of the better known pitfalls in spiritual counseling. The problem will only be intensified if the minister conveys the impression that suicide is a sin and that all who commit the act go straight to hell. If the considerable psychological pain of a survivor or a person at high risk is re-interpreted as a spiritual quest and dealt with only by using such techniques as Bible study, this can also be detrimental to the person. This is not to suggest that the spiritual has no value. But there are times when very focused professional help is needed. If this help is not given the person will not live long enough to appreciate the value of prayer and Bible study.

Discussion

Suicide is one of those topics seldom or never mentioned openly in the church today. Many "popular" churches place major emphasis on the positive, on "feeling good." Suicide can not be discussed from the perspective of a feel-good mentality. It is a very painful, traumatic event. A review of some of the highlights around the topic as presented in this chapter should stimulate more discussion of how the Christian experience of hope and faith can be meaningfully applied in a realistic confrontation with suicide behavior.

Those who work as counselors in the field of suicide have developed skills in two areas. First, they are able to identify the factors pointing to high risk for suicide. The most important of these factors are outlined in Chapter 10. Secondly, these professionals have developed a general theoretical perspective from which to view suicide. Chapter 10 introduces a psycho-dynamic and a behavioral approach to suicide. I see some relevance in both of these approaches but more practical value in the behavioral approach which looks at suicide as another kind of behavior subject to behavioral modification. One way to reduce the risk of suicide is to remove the real or anticipated rewards of the behavior. Another technique is to reward and reinforce positive, life-celebrating behavior.

Some would attempt to re-interpret intervention strategies to infuse them at all points with Christian belief and teaching. I do not see the need for this. The spiritual dimension is real and is powerful on its own merits. There should be no conflict between good counseling and the best of the long heritage of the church. It is possible for someone to go through a secular counseling experience and gain control over a suicide situation. But the process of gaining wholeness is enhanced by touching the resources of God's grace.

Chapter 6
"I Hear Voices"

A few years ago while working for a major unversity as a sociologist I completed a research project that included days of participant observation in a halfway house for people not able to live independently because of schizophrenia or some other form of "mental illness." It was interesting to sit with these men and women as they watched soap operas on TV. There was time to talk with each person and opportunity to observe comings and goings throughout the day.

These people did manifest behavior normally associated with mental illness. But I was also impressed by the many ways in which they demonstrated very normal aspirations. One man owned an old car parked in the street near the facility. He wanted to get this car working again and talked about a trip to Alaska. This line of interest was interspersed with times when he talked to himself, smiling at some kind of message hidden from me. Another man was passing around several issues of Playboy magazine one afternoon. I learned that he had taken most of his meager monthly allowance for personal needs and spent it on the magazines.

A halfway house for the mentally ill would not be selected as a place to find high spiritual aspirations but I did see evidence of this part of life as well. One of the residents was blind. He was very well educated and at one time held a prominent professional position. I was told that the blindness came as one result of a self-inflicted gun shot wound from an attempted suicide. This suicide attempt on his part followed the murder of his wife, a traumatic event which he could not cope with. The dual crisis experiences pushed him "over the edge" and he needed intensive residential care.

I noticed two special characteristics of this man. He seemed to be very concerned about others. I watched one morning as he sat patiently working with a young resident who wanted to get the GED certification. The blind man served as a volunteer tutor. He was very adept at mathematics. He also talked about the Bible and how important prayer was for him. As a social science researcher at that time I thought that it was unfortunate that no minister ever visited this halfway house. This resident and others would have appreciated such a presence. The building was not far from a church I attended. No one on the staff of that church knew about this special part of the community. The residents were not seen as potential church members.

On a more personal level, one of my brothers is schizophrenic. He had his schizophrenic break when he was in his early teens while I was away from home in my first year of college. Over the years my brother has been in and out of state mental hospitals and an assortment of special living situations. He has never been able to function for long without heavy medication and the presence of counselors. My parents have carried the daily concern for his welfare year after year. The family is devoted to the church. My brother talks at times about attending church services and has been taken to church meetings by my folks. One of my regrets over the years is that none of the pastors who have known the family has taken the time to visit my brother. I do not think that participation in a formal service of worship would be advisable because of his difficulty in handling such a group scene. But contact with his situation could have opened up new channels of meaningful communication with my parents.

Schizophrenia is one of the most baffling of the conditions falling within the general category of mental illness. Although programs of ministry can not be expected to generate in-depth research on the fine details of the clinical complications in mental illness specialized ministries including late-night street ministry do become involved with individuals who are mentally ill. In many congregations family members struggle with the problems of someone who has been institutionalized at some time or who is presently a patient in a facility for the mentally ill. This chapter is intended to serve as an introduction to the challenging work of ministry to this often neglected portion of the community.

Background

Who Needs Help?

On the streets of the city I often see very disturbed people. Few would question their need for professional help. This highly visible part of the problem can, however, become a barrier to treatment when the condition is much less severe. One of the difficulties for the mental health professional is that many people equate any form of "counseling" with the stigma of being "crazy." It is not unusual for "normal" people to go through very uncomfortable times including major crisis events during which professional counseling would be beneficial. Too often individuals carry the trauma alone, pushing the feelings deeper within for possible profound dysfunction at some later time.

One of the encouraging developments in recent years has been the growth of self-help groups. There was a time when peer support around a problem was almost synonymous with AA. Now people with problems other than chemical dependency can find people with the same problem(s) and gain mutual reinforcement toward wholeness. Sometimes these groups adopt the 12 steps and other language of AA. A church in Seattle has 12-step groups meeting around such diverse problems as overeating and smoking.

Most of the professional work in counseling does not involve schizophrenic patients. One popular problem area concerns interpersonal relationships. Marital counseling is an example of this type of counseling. Although not often recognized as a form of "counseling" the opportunities to talk about relationships in the informal groups tied to a given church can be beneficial for those involved in a painful cycle of interaction.

I have concern, however, about the "cell" group meetings in homes announced as Bible study groups where intimate and/or traumatic experiences are freely shared. There are times when emotionally charged experiences are best shared with a professional, not a circle of peers. This is especially true for someone who has had intensive counseling or who is now going through such an experience with a professional.

Schizophrenia

Schizophrenia is a very costly, often neglected disease. It is estimated that there are over one million Americans suffering with this disability. Every year some 43,000 new cases are diagnosed. The cost to the country including welfare payments and lost wages amounts to well over $20 billion a year. This disease is chronic, generally leaving the patient unable to pay medical costs. One of the major problems is the adequate monitoring of medication and effective professional intervention through which many schizophrenics can live relatively normal lives and hold jobs.

The most bizarre manifestations of schizophrenia are generally used to define the disease. This does help to indicate the possible types of feelings/states of rationality but can pull attention away from the less stereotypical manifestations and the fairly normal behavior of someone under controlled medications with adequate social support. Schizophrenia was described in great detail by Eugen Bleuler in 1906. He coined the word from the Greek to suggest the breakdown of the mind's unity. As he described the condition, the minds of schizophrenics operate in bits and pieces which distorts reality, muddies perception and loosens the link between cognitive states.

An article appearing in *Science* in 1982 gives a good popular over-view of the early work in schizophrenia. (This article was excerpted by Joann Ellison Rodgers in *The Sunday Denver Post* for September 12, 1982.) As the author indicates, the disease generally strikes in adolescence or young adulthood and lasts a life time. Grandiose illusions can accompany the disease. Nijinsky, a famous ballet dancer, was described as schizophrenic in 1919 at the age of 29. During one schizophrenic episode he wrote . . . "Nijinsky has faults, but Nijinsky must be listened to because he speaks the words of God . . . I am God, Nijinsky is God." After the diagnosis of schizophrenia Nijinsky never danced again.

The *Science* article also describes a contemporary case of schizophrenia to illustrate the nature of the disease. A young man by the name of Franz who is 23 says he is a "riddle of bones." He hears buzzing voices, penetrating squeals and voices with messages he sometimes understands but cannot remember. He sees flashes of light and shadow in the middle of the room. He says that strangers can send their shadows to visit him in bed. He chews his tie, hoards garbage, sits in a stupor for weeks and hits his nurses. Occasionally, he clowns and walks on his hands.

Another look at schizophrenia is offered by the following lengthy excerpt from an insightful article appearing in the *Seattle Times* of April 26, 1982:

When she was Johann Sebastian Bach or Moses, she spoke in detail of her life as a composer or biblical leader. Frequently she became so worried about the poor of the world that she assumed their identity because she felt better able to cope with their problems. Her special mission was to help the helpless.

Her visions were of angels or historical figures. The voices in her head told her to carry on their good works. That was on the better days. More often, the voices harangued her relentlessly. They told her she was a worthless person. They told her she was being watched.

At times, she believed an entire city followed her wherever she went. Once after visiting the zoo, she suffered severe headaches because she believed a horse had replaced her brain with its brain, and it was too big for her skull.

139

At the root of it all, she believed, were her ancestors. They were the voices who told her she had a heavy responsibility to carry on for them. She once was petrified that physicians performing a spinal tap would penetrate her backbone with the needle and kill her ancestors who "live there." Another time, she was enraged when hospital clinicians urged her to stop putting her finger in her nose. More ancestors lived there and it was her duty to stroke them, she said.

In real life, she was her parents' prized daughter. They pressured her to excel. They wanted her to be a superachiever in memory of relatives who had been killed in Nazi concentration camps. In real life, the young woman did excel. Though the mental illness first began to torment her at age 19, she struggled through college and earned a master's degree from a prestigious university. She held a highly responsible job until she no longer could fight the voices in her mind alone.

Her father desperately hoped treatment in the mental hospital would help. But he often said in her presence that if she didn't get well, she was worthless to everyone. Hitler, he said, was correct in advocating euthanasia for the mentally ill.

Through it all, the young woman was fully aware that she was ill and at times was able to think quite clearly. For instance, she sometimes made "absolutely astute observations" about others in her therapy group.

Imagine the pain she feels when she's alert and aware . . . It's absolutely amazing she's able to do as well as she does," says Dr. Robert Waters, who treated the woman in another state and has since become Director of Harborview Center's new schizophrenia program. No successful treatment was found for the woman and she still is hospitalized.

That often is the case for those with one of the most devastating human illnesses: schizophrenia. (Warren King, The Seatle Times, April 26, 1982.)

The "Space Case"

Since this book has a strong interest in problems on the city streets some mention of the so-called "space case" (Segal, Baumohl and Johnson, 1977) is called for. The term is used in some cities to refer to people with chronic mental disorders who wander the streets as part of the homeless population. The homeless mentally ill fall through the cracks in existing services. In places like Los Angeles I have heard professionals from helping agencies talk about the reality that there is no "safety net," no effective network to "fall through."

Social margin is essential for personal survival. Most times we all act like we are expected to act. We help others, obey the rules, do our job and get rewarded with good things like money. The space case (a term used on the street, not a professional designation of people) by contrast, has either an inability or an unwillingness to comply with social role expectations. Such a person may also engage in a deliberate manipulation of role expectations for immediate gain only to loose long-term professional help. Because of a long-standing pattern of not complying with standard expectations the space case does not have social margin when help is needed. Social margin would include resources, relationships and a credible identity with family, community services and peers.

From a distance one might assume that a space case could find ready acceptance among "street people." But this is not always the case. In recent years drug use and drug dealing have come to dominate the sub-culture of the street. Someone with obvious problems of mental illness will not be included in the social system where drugs determine relationships. The following quotation illustrates the attitude of the drug dealer toward a space case. It suggests a degree of alienation which cries out for understanding and social support.

Space cases, man are crazy y-know? You can't trust em. Not y'know because they're dishonest or nothin'. But they just don't know what they're doing most of the time.

141

You can't sell 'em nothin' y'know put 'em in business
'cause they'll just get busted. And maybe you with 'em
. . . The best thing to do is just shine 'em on. Not even
let 'em know you got nothin', y'know; if a space case
asks to buy some acid, y'know, I say "what acid?" You
don't want to let em in 'cause then they'll be bringing
you customers. I mean all sorts of weird space cases'd
be comin' by if they know you got something. Bringing
God knows who at all sorts of times, and just wantin'
two joints, or maybe two hits or something, y'know? It
ain't worth it.
(Segal, et. al., 1977, p. 389)

One difficulty in looking primarily at the people "out there" and how their behavior only serves to get them into more trouble is that the system which is designed to respond to the homeless mentally ill is also often in disarray. People living on the street see rules and regulations as inconsistent and confusing and often times they are. People are put in the position where they must prove that they are crazy in order to survive. Their craziness is documented in a case record. Mental heath professionals are submerged with paper work. One agency rountinely accumulates 34 pieces of paper on a single client after only three months of contact. An administrator in this mental health agency claims that it is the delivery of mental health services which is really crazy! One reason a space case individual lives on the street is that he/she is either unable or unwilling to go through the bureaucratic process of filling out forms and keeping interview appointments to get regular support checks. A serendipitous benefit or one that may be actually planned is that there is a certain amount of protection in being labeled as "crazy." Strangers are less likely to attack someone who appears to be totally incapacitated.

One area in which the mental health system is particularly vulnerable involves responses to people with more than one major presenting problem. It is not unusual for a person with a history of chronic mental illness to also be an alcoholic or a drug addict, for example. Such a person may not be able to find a counselor in a community mental health center who has a background in chemical dependency. If this person goes to an alcohol/drug treatment program he/she is very unlikely to get mental health counseling. Professionals working in the field of chemical dependency may have very little respect for the importance of medications for chronic mental illness. Such medications may, in fact, be seen as simply another form of dependency which the person must become free from. This approach can have a devastating impact upon the stability of the schizophrenic.

The idea of a dual diagnosis has been used most often with reference to people with mental illness who become addicted to illegal drugs and alcohol. A newer development is the phenomenon of people using drugs who then begin to show symtoms of mental illness. In the reference to drug addicts in Chapter 4 an experience with a man who suddenly disappeared to give himself a shot of cocaine with a needle was described. This was a strong lesson in the modification of behavior for me. Before the cocaine dose this man seemed normal, perhaps a little on the mellow side. After the cocaine took effect he changed dramaticaly. A paranoid condition seemed to grip him. He locked the door of the motel room, pulled a chair up under the door knob and closed the drapes. I also watched as he picked at the metal grating of the heating unit on the wall of the room. It was as if he heard threatening voices or noises coming out of the inert piece of metal. Professionals in the field tell me that it is not unusual for a person on cocaine to experience acute episodes of paranoia. Sometimes there is a conviction that danger is coming from the sky. Other times the person will pick up a small object like a piece of wood and stare it down like something possessed. State hospital admissions now include an increasing number of people diagnosed as mentally ill only after experience with drugs.

Personal Glimpses

"I Have Committed the Unpardonable Sin"

In Portland, Oregon, I had several contacts with a middle-aged man who seemed very lonely. As I recall he talked about church attendance. He lived in one of the cheap downtown hotels. I saw him on the street or in a small store which sold a limited number of basic food items to folks living near Burnside Street. After I became acquainted with this man he told me that he was once a patient at the State Hospital. He felt that he was doing fairly well on his own.

One day he seemed very depressed as he came near me and began to talk. He wanted me to know that he had "committed the unpardonable sin." His total emotional tone was changed in contrast to previous meetings. I mention this particular person because it gives me an opportunity to suggest a response which is not the best. At the time of this last meeting with the man I was with a local pastor whom I wanted to become involved in the program of street ministry. I responded to my friend on the street in a way which I thought might impress the pastor. I treated the man's problem as a spiritual problem. Since he mentioned sin I elaborated on this and ended the contact with a prayer for him. A few days later I did not see him in his normal haunts. When I made inquiry at his hotel I was told that his case manager had come around and that he was again back in the State Hospital. Immediately prior to the hospitalization he was fighting delusions so desperately that he crawled under his bed and refused to come out. He had not been taking his medications. I should have encouraged him to see his case manager and should have asked about medications.

Coffee and Deep Depression

In an all-night restaurant in St. Louis I ordered hot chocolate at the counter one night and then sat near others who were having coffee. A waitress told me that a young woman sitting across the room seemed very disturbed. I went over to this woman and sat down opposite her at a small table. She immediately started talking to me about her situation. She said that she had been living on her own recently and felt that this had been going fairly well. But over the last couple of days she started going into a state of deep depression. She was thinking of suicide. She also said that she had been a patient at the State Hospital. I became very directive with this woman, saying something like "It sounds to me like you need to go back to the hospital." She agreed to go. I called the hospital. They pulled the woman's record and told me to bring her out. I completed this chance encounter by driving the woman to the hospital and watching as they re-admitted her.

"I'm a Manic-Depressive"

In St. Louis I often walked through both the Greyhound and Trailways Bus Depots. One night I watched as a well-dressed man in his mid-50s paced the floor from one end of the Greyhound Depot to the other. I walked over to him and introduced myself. He said that his name was Jim, that he was from Ohio and that he was going out to California as part of some major enterprise. Then he went on about his past experiences as a college professor of history. He took out his wallet to show me identification cards from Blue Cross insurance and for membership in an association of people with manic depression. This became the introduction to his major problem at the time; he was going through a spell of acute agitation as part of his mental illness.

Given his high level of education and intelligence, Jim was in touch with both his problem and appropriate professional intervention. He informed me that he wanted to talk with someone in a clinic which had connections with the Manic-Depressive Association. I did not know how to evaluate the availability of options at that hour of the night. I called one of the major local hospitals which had a special psychiatric

145

unit. Jim hesitated about going there when I could not give him strong assurances about how they might respond to a manic-depressive. But after some discussion and with his rising state of agitation he agreed to take a chance. He felt that he could not just spend the night pacing the floor in a strange downtown bus depot.

The trip across town was one of those "unusual" experiences. I decided to pull out onto the freeway system which circles the city of St. Louis. After only a mile or two the far right lane came to an abrupt halt. Ahead red lights were flashing and a uniformed officer was directing traffic around the scene of an accident. I pulled over, stopped and ran ahead on foot to see if there was anything I could do. Jim sat in the front seat, his arms and legs moving in a rhythmic swaying of nervous tension. My help was not needed at the crash site. We hurried on to the hospital, pulled up into the emergency entrance zone and walked inside. Unfortunately, this hospital did not have a psychiatric specialist on duty. We left and drove to a second hospital some distance away.

In this second hospital I walked with Jim down long halls to a general reception area. After waiting for our turn we were informed that a resident in psychiatry was on duty and that he could see Jim. This resident did a very good job. He talked with Jim and then with both of us together. He went into the details of medication and he also got the name of Jim's psychiatrist in Ohio. The Ohio psychiatrist gave specific instructions about the best course of treatment for Jim. The most immediate need was for emergency shelter. On the following day plans were made for Jim to return home. The hospital maintained a transportation system for all patients including those seen in the emergency room. When I was assured that they would follow-up on the need for a return trip downtown to a shelter I left the hospital and returned to the streets for more work. I was so impressed with the excellent work of this hospital that I sent a letter to the man in charge of the psychiatric unit. His reply was very disturbing to me. He was very condescending to me, a lowly minister. He questioned the process of daring to imply that psychiatric services could be rated from poor to good or excellent. His strong message to me was that it was none of my business how well his professionals were doing, they *always* did excellent! When I read his letter I found myself wishing that he could confront the mental health system late at night in different cities as I have done. It might indeed look very comfortable from where he sits but for people on the street it is simply not something which can be taken as a given.

"I Am Jesus"

I was working in St. Louis before the City Hospital was moved to its present location some distance from the immediate downtown area. Back then the hospital was across the street from the city's mental hospital, Malcolm Bliss. This created problems when patients who needed mental health care ended up at the wrong hospital. One night a young woman who seemed to be in a very severe state of confusion was waiting in the room adjacent to the emergency entrance at the City Hospital.

I was able to initiate interaction with this woman. One of her problems was that she could not get the receptionist to understand her. I volunteered to go up to the intake window with her to help answer questions. The person doing intake for the hospital was very annoyed when the young woman began to struggle over such simple questions as "most recent address." At one point this hospital employee yanked the forms out of her typewriter with an oath and yelled that she had to account for "every carbon copy" she made. It did not take long to discover that the woman trying to get help was really at the wrong hospital. She should have been across the street at the city's mental hospital. The police had dropped her off at the wrong hospital.

My next move was to walk the woman over to Malcolm Bliss. I waited with her in the waiting room. She smoked one cigarette after another. Then she fell asleep, leaning against me. When she woke up she looked at me and said that she was Jesus. I was glad when her name was finally called and she left the waiting room for her interview with the resident on duty.

I assumed that my work would be over after the intake interview. Surely this very disturbed young woman would be taken in for the night at least. But that was not to be the case. When she appeared again in the waiting room I asked to see the resident who had interviewed her. He had done some probing of her delusions. But he never covered the basics of where she was living and never gave any consideration to where she might stay that night. I was very angry at this turn of events. I thought that her immediate need for shelter should have been given some priority. Although she was not really the kind of person who would do well in a regular shelter because of her mental illness I decided that I would try to find her a place to spend the night. I drove her to a shelter not far from the hospital. A knock on the door and the ringing of a door bell finally aroused someone. But they had no room for another guest. After getting the same response from another emergency shelter I took the young woman back to the waiting room of the mental hospital, informing her that she might need to sit up in this room all night. It was around 2:30 a.m. when I left her. I could do no more because I had to get a little sleep before an early morning meeting.

Trying to Get Into the State Hospital

My encounter with Jill is reported in Chapter 1. This is the young woman I found in a general hospital waiting room around midnight. The hospital found no reason for admission. Jill had hitchhiked from a nearby city to get herself admitted into the state hospital. I drove her to the appropriate local screening hospital for emergency admissions but she refused to remain until the clinicians could examine her. I was told

148

that she was a "system abuser." But this did not solve her immediate problem of being stranded in a strange city far from friends and her own apartment.

This young woman wore a brace on one leg and walked with a limp from a childhood illness. She was one of the mentally ill but could function within limits most of the time when regularly taking her medication.

As I have indicated elsewhere in this book, the role of the minister is seldom clearly defined. I was not a mental health professional. What should I do to help this stranger late at night? I decided to offer to drive her back to her place of residence. She had no funds. At 2:00 a.m., emergency shelter would be hard to arrange. She would need to ultimately return to her own city. As I shared in Chapter 1, I not only drove her back to her own city but several miles beyond to take her to a hospital which had helped her in the past. She was admitted at this hospital. It was an all-night vigil for me.

Snakes in The Cup

On one of the nights when I started my rounds by dropping into an emergency shelter on Burnside Street in Portland, Oregon a middle-aged man saw my clergy collar and immediately came over to stand near me. He was very anxious as he explained to me that snakes were coming out of the empty coffee cup he was holding. He also informed me confidentially that FBI agents were after him. He was homeless but could not remain in the shelter because of his extreme fear that people in the place were trying to kill him. This man was very serious about his paranoid delusions. It would have been futile to have attempted a direct attack on his images. I listened and wondered why he trusted me.

This stranger asked if he could walk around with me all night. I told him that I would not be out all night but invited him to leave the shelter with me as I headed west on Burnside Street back to downtown Portland. As we walked along in the

149

dark I learned a little more about my new friend. He was not unfamiliar with institutional care and expressed a desire to see someone that night. I knew that the University of Oregon Hospital system was in the habit of accepting mentally ill patients for screeening if these patients appeared in person in the emergency room. I did not know how I could get this man to the hospital since I did not have a car in town. I had taken the bus down from Seattle for the weekend.

I did have $10 in cash as my total reserve to cover my expenses the rest of the night plus any needs later in the day as I rode the early morning bus back to Seattle. This would be a four-hour bus trip for me. I called a local cab and asked the driver what he would charge to take my friend to the hospital. He said that he could make the trip for $5. I held the back door open for the stranger and wished him well as I handed a $5 bill to the driver of the cab.

It was with a sense of minor accomplishment but also a feeling of uneasiness about my friend that I walked away from the cab to pay a visit in the worst Skid Road hotel I have ever seen. This place in Portland was the "black hole of Calcutta." Late-stage alcoholics stayed in rooms only a little larger than animal stalls. There were no conventional doors on the individual "rooms," only thin boards with cheap padlocks. Chicken wire was stretched across the top of these spaces for a makeshift ceiling. The lobby area of this "hotel" was sometimes smeared with the trail of human feces. The inside of any given room was often a complete litter of empty beer cans and wine bottles. The talk of hotel residents often included references to things like "a Volkswagon the size of an elephant."

Perhaps one can picture at least some of the setting into which I walked when I made a call at this place. I went there not because of the filth and the agony of alcoholism but because I felt that the night clerk enjoyed my presence. I chatted with him about his trips to Alaska in former years and about an aunt who was a missionary. On this particular night after my experience with the stranger who was paranoid it happened to be a few days before Christmas. The desk clerk surprised me by announcing that he had a Christmas present for me. He left the desk, went to his room in the hotel and came back with his gift, handing it to me with a smile. I was given a small pocket flashlight which was wrapped in a $20 bill! I was totally surprised that this hotel would be the place for such generosity. I spent $5 on a stranger and was given $20 by another stranger, all within 45 minutes!

Eating at King's Table

I mentioned earlier in this chapter that one of my brothers is schizophrenic. I have not always lived within driving distance of him so there have been years during which my only contact came during occasions like summer vacations. For the past few years he has lived in a halfway house maintained by the state. This is perhaps the best living arrangement he has ever had. He is given considerable freedom including the freedom to clutter his room if he wants. Counselors are available and medication is monitored. One day a week he goes to a building separate from his living facility where he is given a few simple chores to do. This might include the emptying of ash trays, for example.

One of his obvious pleasures is to eat out, preferably at a smorgasbord type cafeteria called King's Table. On occasion my brother, father and I have shared the experience of lunch together. My brother is given the freedom to load his own tray. He always piles it high with most everything in sight. At the table he leaves a trail of vegetables and mashed potatoes between the tray and his lap. Pieces of the food get caught in his beard which is graying now. His fingernails are long. His hair is matted and stringy. Sometimes he takes part in the conversation. At other times he takes off into a world of his own, going on about things like "I could make $1,000 a day selling Tupperware" or "there's a mud wall around the whole universe, Christians go to heaven where they build flying saucers."

151

I am sure that anyone looking at my brother would immediately write him off as "one of those." This is unfortunate because he has some very good qualities if one sees him as a person first. I am often amazed by the way he remembers small details of family life I have long ago forgotten. He will ask about someone, remembering them by name. One of my fondest experiences with my schizophrenic brother came during one of the spells shortly after finishing college when I was looking for work. This came at a time when he was actually trying to hold down a job. For a few days he worked for a company that cleaned carpets. When he heard that I needed a job he invited me to go with him. I don't remember the outcome of that contact. I do remember my brother showing me how to work a carpet cleaner. Those few days were the only days of regular work he has ever known.

One of the most regretable parts of his long experience with schizophrenia is that he was diagnosed back when the "treatment" was much more radical than it is today. He was a patient back in the "locked wards" era of mental illness. While I was going to college he was getting regular electric shock treatments. Recently I interviewed a young woman in her 20s who is schizophrenic. She was aware of the specific medications she was taking, was attending a day treatment program, was very well groomed and looking forward to semi-independent living. I could not help but contrast her case with the major deficits which my brother will always carry.

Reactions

I am a little uncomfortable about the reactions to mental illness which are suggested in the previous pages. For alcohol and drug addiction the "reactions" are more likely to be part of a total transformation of life. Chronic mental illness is not subject to such a drastic transformation. Maybe this is why I include references to counseling in general as well as references to conditions such as schizophrenia. The reactions to mental illness which are most likely to be found in programs of street ministry are listed below. Sometimes these same reactions are found in other programs of ministry.

Giving the Person Space

There are times on the street when a stranger makes it clear that he/she does not want me near. Perhaps a mental health worker would force the issue. But I feel no compulsion to do this. I give the person space. This person has the right to tell me to back off.

Dealing With Failure

I am not always successful in trying to minister to someone with a chronic pattern of mental illness. I am thinking, for example, of a woman who seemed so agitated when I first saw her that I suggested she contact a mental health center. This was not the kind of information she wanted. She started ranting and raving about how I was "a hypocrite" and a "no good." I attempted to calm her but could not. There were other calls from this woman. For a time she called me on the telephone several times a night. I finally told her that she could not go on with this behavior. Then she got mad again. At no point did I feel that I had really been a positive influence on this woman. After she was picked up by the police and taken to jail because of the charges leveled by someone else I learned that she had been going without her medication for two years.

Networking with Other Agencies

One of the most important aspects of street ministry is to be able to contact other agencies. As the personal glimpses suggest, it is not always possible to immediately resolve a dilemma in trying to help someone with a long-standing pattern of mental illness. It is always important to know local resources. The schizophrenic must be given encouragement to continue on the medications which are prescribed. Most cities have a total system of services for the mentally ill from drop-in daytime centers to crisis outreach. One of the major problems is that a person can play off one helping resource against another while not really receiving the kind of professional help needed. Programs of ministry including street ministry must not become a kind of doormat for soaking up problems and not facing up to the difficult decisions even the mentally ill must make.

Giving Practical Help

One strong advantage in programs of street ministry is that a clergy person is on the scene, capable of giving immediate practical help. If the situation calls for it someone can be transported to the emergency room of a hospital or to some other facility. Or a person who feels threatened can be escorted back to his/her place of residence. Other times the real need is for money to make a telephone call. When confused and in a strange city the person who is mentally ill may need help in accessing the available emergency shelter system.

Responding to Crisis Events

With appropriate medication, social support and back up counseling systems the person with chronic mental illness can maintain himself on a fairly normal level. But crisis times will occur. This may come, for example, during a period when the person is not taking prescribed medications for some reason or when there are major changes in that person's family. A street minister and clergy people in general can be a major resource during times of crisis. The most immediate concern is to identify the situation as a crisis, a time out of the ordinary for some reason. Another paramount issue is the ability to make a referral and/or direct personal contact with the appropriate professional resource for the crisis. In the scenarios from the street I report times when I helped people get to emergency rooms for evaluation. As part of crisis management the ideal would be to help the individual grow in his/her own management of crisis events.

Knowing the Appropriate Place for Special Spiritual Ministry

I shared the experience of a very inappropriate handling of the spiritual touch in my account of the man who really needed to get back on his medication. There are times when prayer and Scripture are appropriate. But used inappropriately these touchstones of the faith may only add confusion by turning attention away from the more critical acute mental health needs at the time.

I have indicated that people with chronic mental illness often have spiritual aspirations but seldom find reinforcement within the established church. We must find better ways to communiate with special populations including the mentally ill. A program of chaplaincy in a mental hospital I am familiar with is very limited in offering only a standard church service on the premises. This does have some value. But I wonder what might be possible if we took each person more seriously, trying to capture his/her own struggles with faith and hope. Maybe elements of a traditional church service would be useful. But there would also be an incorporation of other elements, making both the formal worship time and the one-on-one contacts in ministry different because those being served have special needs.

Discussion

Today as I walked toward my office downtown I passed a woman who was sitting on a concrete bench immediately in front of the entrance to the building where I work. It is a cold December day. This woman wears only a thin jacket. I stopped to speak to her. Her responses to me indicated serious problems in the handling of normal social exchanges, characteristic of one who is mentally impaired. I assume that this woman is a resident in one of the nearby halfway houses. Or perhaps she is someone who will be going to a day-treatment program in the city.

What should be the response of the church to the mentally ill? Their presence in a church service can be disruptive. I am thinking of a young man who regularly attends a church I attend. He is given special attention by people of the church. During the coffee hour, for example, a table is set up just for him so that he will not spill coffee and sugar all over the main serving table. He will sometimes come to church late, take his place and then walk in and out while the service is in process.

One of the most promising forms of ministry to the mentally ill is the work now going on in different cities on the streets with people on their own turf. This is the kind of approach which is recommended by many professionals in the mental health field. Much of the stigma which accompanies mental illness loses its impact in the immediacy of a personal encounter late at night. Talk with a stranger on the street will be around common things such as shelter. There is no need to first give a clinical assessment before becoming involved. Many times I have chatted with people with no awareness that they have a formal diagnosis of mental illness. It is important to respond to the real concern of others, treating them first as people instead of forcing them into a pre-set category.

The additional information in Chapter 11 should be helpful in giving a brief over-view of such topics as "psychotherapy." Since this book is close to actual situations on the street the emphasis on these pages is on some of the practical approaches including reality therapy and a customer model of care. These approaches have importance far beyond the world of the downtown streets at night.

Chapter 7
Preaching the Gospel in the City

During the day most large cities become a beehive of activity. Shoppers, office workers, tourists and others rush from place to place. Cities like New York have been immortalized by photographs of people marching like cattle along a packed sidewalk. But most of these people return home to the suburbs late in the afternoon. It is surprising to see the shift in the downtown atmosphere at night. Streets become deserted. Even with street lights in place a darkness settles over the sidewalk in many places. Neon lights identify hotels and taverns. The profile of tall buildings may be outlined by artistically placed flood lights. The activity of the night centers around hotel lobbies, taverns, cocktail lounges, bus depots, hospital emergency rooms and sidewalks.

The combination of darkness and downtown can be very threatening. It is easier to have faith and trust in others when the sun is shining. Most of us have had experiences of fear as we have listened to the uncertain sounds of the night, in the city or far away from the city while hiking or camping out. There are times when fears at night become blown all out of proportion resulting in devastating consequences. This becomes a major theme in the popular novel, *Lord of the Flies*, (1954) by William Golding, the story of a group of boys lost on an island who overreact to the sounds and sights of the night.

Where does ministry fit in this picture? When people think of the church and the city they generally think only of "inner city" ministry, not of the downtown core of the city. Inner city work is done with low-income people who may have major problems due in part to racial and ethnic barriers. The inner city is a community. Over the years dedicated clergy have become seriously involved in inner city projects. This often includes moving into the inner city and adopting in part the lifestyle of those who will be served. Inner city work may involve late-night street ministry. But the day-time contacts are more critical. A minister in the inner city must be known by the total system which becomes his/her parish. There are few settings for ministry with more challenges and more opportunity for Christian witness.

But the "inner city" is not the primary focus of this book. I propose a consideration of another part of the city, the downtown "core" area or "central business district." Downtown does not have the kind of social system structure which typifies the "inner-city." Downtown changes drastically from the day-time hours to night-time. In the downtown core there are more chance encounters with strangers. There are also some of the most difficult kinds of problems because the core of any city attracts people in transit, those recently released from jail and people who are drawn to the anonymity which the center of the city offers.

Downtown, one-on-one ministry is championed in the work of Jesus. The Scripture passage I use often as a prelude to talking about my work is the account of Jesus touching blind Bartimaeus as recorded in the Gospel of Mark, Chapter 10, verses 46 to 52:

> *And they came to Jericho: and as he went out from Jericho with his disciples and a great multitude, Bartimaeus, a blind beggar, the son of Timaeus, was sitting by the way side. And when he heard that it was Jesus of Nazareth, he began to cry out and say, Jesus Son of David, have mercy on me. And many rebuked him, telling him to be quiet. But he cried out all the more saying, Son of David have mercy on me. And Jesus stopped and said call him. And they called the blind man, saying to him, be of good cheer, rise, he is calling you. And throwing off his mantle he sprung up and came to Jesus. And Jesus said to him, What do you want me to do for you? And he said to him, Master, let me receive my sight. And Jesus said to him, Go your way, Your faith has made*

159

you well. And immediately he received his sight and
followed him on the way.
Mark, Ch. 10: 46-52, ASV.

As I interpret this passage of Scripture I imagine Jesus on his way to some important meeting but stopping in the process to reach out in love to one person. That person is not one of the most sought after citizens of the city. He is in fact a lowly blind beggar, one of the "lepers" of his day. Street ministry must stop to touch others on their own turf. This special commission must continue as a powerful extension of the work begun so long ago by our Lord.

The over-riding concern for spiritual ministry must not rule out the need to look at some very practical issues. Downtown ministry proceeds best when there is keen appreciation for the nature of the city environment.

The Downtown Setting

Sidewalks: More Than A Place to Walk

People who work downtown use the sidewalks as a way to get from one place to another. For them there is no hidden meaning in any one part of the sidewalk compared to another. But anyone who spends most of his/her time on the streets must develop a much more sophisticated approach to sidewalks. As a beginning such a person needs to know where certain types of people "hang out." Some corners are known as the turf for drug dealers. Other sidewalk areas are locations for street prostitutes. In Tacoma and other cities the sidewalk spaces for male prostitutes are different than the spaces generally used by female prostitutes. In cities like Los Angeles there are strong rules of territoriality around sidewalk spaces. These rules are enforced by gang members who are not afraid of using lethal force against any conscious or unconscious violation of turf claims.

The notion of sidewalk use as part of illicit trafficking is only a small part of the importance of sidewalks for "street people." An intimate familiarity with the city's streets will include knowledge of small places where one can hide in out of the rain. Sidewalks are also identified in terms of degree of friendliness and safety from the threat of police arrest. What seems like a small distance for anyone who regularly drives a car downtown can be a major social and psychological distance for a street person. I once asked a drug addict/dealer to meet me in a coffee shop one block from the drug scene in one city. This was a coffee shop which I often went to. But it was out of bounds for this person. She did not know the place and made it obvious that she would not feel comfortable going there.

Sidewalks invite the use of the term "make-do" as coined by the sociologist Erving Goffman. He used the term to refer to the practice of using something for a purpose for which it was not originally intended. In the book *You Owe Yourself a Drunk* (1970) anthropologist James Spradley gives the story of a man who often sat in a Seattle tavern drinking until the early morning hours. Back then it was the practice for the police to routinely pick up "drunks," taking them directly to jail. To avoid arrest the man in Spradley's book staggered to the nearest small park in downtown Seattle and crawled in under the bushes until the morning light to avoid arrest. The park was only a few blocks from his hotel but he did not want to risk an arrest. This small park space immediately off the sidewalk was not designed to be a haven for winos. Its use by the wino for this purpose was a form of "make-do" behavior. Another example of such behavior would be the common practice of using a bus stop bench as a place to camp out. If the bus stop has a roof and some kind of side barrier against the wind and rain it easily becomes an emergency shelter for periods during the day, at night and/or all night unless the person using it is told to "move along" by a police officer.

I have known shopping bag ladies who regularly do all of their personal laundry in the public restrooms of downtown bus depots. All of these are examples of the kind of behavior which Erving Goffman described as "make-do."

One of the more recent additions to the long list of make-dos on the downtown streets involves the use of restrooms in late-night restaurants and taverns. These facilities are obviously intended for very specific purposes. But at night and during the day it is easy for them to become places where people inject drugs and/or sell drugs. A night place which has only a limited work crew is most vulnerable to this kind of activity since it becomes impossible to keep a constant eye on who is using the restroom. When anyone disappears into such a restroom for a long period of time this is most likely part of a drug scene. This type of make-do becomes important for the addict as a way to avoid the open display of "works" which might invite the attention of the police and immediate transport to jail.

The street minister must become familiar with the nature of specific downtown sidewalks. Many times it helps to anticipate the kinds of problems which might be encountered. I know, for example, that anyone I see on a specific sidewalk in Tacoma will most likely be involved in drugs as an addict or a pusher. I also know the sidewalks which have a reputation for violence including drive-by shootings. I am also alert to the sight of anyone who appears on a given turf but who does not seem to belong there by his/her clothes and general mannerisms. This out-of-place person could very well be someone who needs special consideration. He/she may be a newcomer or someone who is seriously disoriented. Sometimes a street minister can help by interpreting the scene for such a person. I recall, for example, going into an all-night donut shop in Seattle and seeing a very elderly senior citizen. He lived not far from the shop and liked donuts. He had no idea that this donut shop was the center of drug and prostitution activity. I encouraged him to limit his walks to the daytime hours or at least to walk in another direction at night.

A final comment on sidewalks is necessary. Street ministers give attention to the way they walk on the sidewalk. One way to discourage strangers from approaching is to walk at a fast pace, giving the impression that one is in a hurry to get somewhere. The seasoned street minister will slow the walking pace down, taking many opportunities to say "Hi." The minister must give the impression of being available. I do not think that this is something which can be taught. There is a whole pattern of body language and feelings involved in social interaction. With experience and serious commitment to others in ministry some truly miraculous exchanges can occur.

Taverns and Cocktail Lounges

I am not aware of a manual for ministers which gives specific information about the city's drinking places. Late-night, downtown ministry that is effective will include taverns and cocktail lounges as part of the turf. I know most of these downtown places in six different cities where I have served in ministry. In such a place I usually sit at the bar and order either a soft drink or hot tea. A bar stool is better than a seat around a table away from the bar because the position at the bar is more likely to attract conversation. People who sit at tables are normally considered to be waiting for a friend. Going into a tavern and sitting at the bar while wearing a clergy collar will often spark comments which then become a base for the discussion of many different topics.

One way to characterize taverns and cocktail lounges is to consider the bartender(s). A Skid Road tavern will most likely have a bartender who is not far removed from Skid Road in his/her lifestyle. The lower the social class level of a tavern the more likely it will be operated by a female bartender. These bartenders make very little money and are under a lot of work stress. A gay bar will have a bartender who is gay. A tavern which caters to people who are either socially or mentally marginal will most likely have a bartender of this same type. Going up the scale of places, the more affluent cocktail lounges are more likely to have either male or female bartenders dressed in a semi-formal shirt/tie/black coat ensemble.

Night places vary considerably in degree of physical cleanliness. I have been in places where cockroaches dance across counters. These places may not have an automatic dishwasher. The glasses are dunked in lukewarm water, dried halfheartedly with a dirty cloth and then re-used. This always gives me an uneasy feeling but I do not make a scene by asking for special treatment. One of the worst experiences of feeling that I might pick up someone else's germs came in a tavern on Denver's Skid Road when a prostitute sitting next to me at a bar pushed some half-eaten salad into my mouth. She did not mean to be offensive. But I did not appreciate the gesture.

Factual information about night places and the feelings around such places are both very important in the process of attracting and keeping volunteer clergy for programs of late-night ministry. As I mentioned in Chapter 1, when I first went into the cocktail lounge of a Sheraton Hotel after going into Skid Road taverns I sat and stared at the automatic dishwasher as the clean cocktail glasses were driven through jets of hot, sparkling water and then sent into a drying phase. There wasn't a spot on those high-stemmed glasses as the bartender wearing a black cut-away coat carefully replaced them in an overhead rack. This was such a contrast to the style of a Skid Road place that I almost wanted to pay admission to watch the show.

One of the most detailed studies of the social structure of a cocktail lounge is reported by James Spradley and Barbara Mann in the book *The Cocktail Waitress: Woman's Work in a Man's World* (1975). The book is based on research in a lounge close to a college campus. Although some of the features of this place are different than the features I have seen in other such places there are many similarities. The general approach to social structure is also insightful.

Spradley and Mann describe in some detail the role differentiation between the different social actors in the cocktail lounge. The bartender (male) was the proprietor of the space behind the bar. The cocktail waitress (female) was not permitted to invade his domain. Among the waitresses there were subtle distinctions between the day and night waitresses and the specific turf within the lounge which a given waitress was responsible for. Those who patronized the cocktail lounge were categorized in terms of degree of status as customers. The "real regulars" were customers who came to the lounge on a very frequent basis. These men had considerable influence in the place. The owners consulted with them before hiring new employees. They "owned" particular bar stools and were very resentful if anyone dared to usurp their place.

The next highest category of customer in the study were the "regulars." These were male customers who were openly accepted but who did not have the tenure of the "real regulars." Next came "female customers." The researchers found that all employees of the cocktail lounge including the female waitresses gave female customers a lower ranking than male customers. These female customers were regular patrons of the place. But they were considered to be a nuisance because of some of their behavior such as insisting on individual checks when in a group. Men were regarded as more knowledgeable about how to order drinks and in general about the expectations within the lounge. "People off the street" were placed at the bottom of the status hierarchy. These strangers were much more likely to disrupt established role expectations. They were served drinks but not allowed into the intimate exchanges among regular customers.

I mention this study of the social system of the cocktail lounge to reinforce the idea that a tavern or cocktail lounge has a pre-existing structure which a night minister walks into. It is important to spot the "regular regulars." Like the bartenders, they can be helpful by pointing out people in need if they are convinced of the value of the clergy presence. There is also an opportunity to serve as the chaplain for these people. Some of them become regular regulars because they are alcoholic, consuming large amounts of beer and/or wine during the week. I know some who are always present in a given

165

tavern. They may help around the place by watching for "trouble" as a back-up security presence or even help the bartender serve drinks during a busy time.

I have only recently started going into the night places which feature live bands and a younger crowd of customers. These are places where it is more difficult to minister. The music is loud. On busy nights people dance in very crowded open spaces surrounded by tables full of other customers. Sometimes it is hard to find a place to sit. There may be a cover charge to enter. The lyrics of songs are not taken from a church hymnal. I have been hit by the sharp contrast between suggestive lyrics on a Saturday night and the familiar refrains of hymns on Sunday morning. Although these places are a challenge they are also places where ministry can be important. I have seen the acceptance of clergy over time in such a setting. The key is to maintain a ministry of presence style, not a preaching ministry and to keep in contact week after week.

Bus Depots

In a large city the bus depots are usually open late or all night. They are a good place for ministry because of the wide assortment of people who use them during the evening. There are major and important differences between a depot area in New York City or some other very large city and the "average" bus depot but some features are fairly common. A bus depot often has three major areas for customer use: 1. A place(s) where passengers wait for their bus. This space will generally have seating accommodations and perhaps coin-operated, small TV monitors attached to selected seats. 2. Restaurant and/or cocktail lounge areas intended for both bus passengers and the general public. and 3. Free spaces in-between the above two areas.

The major regular social actors in a bus depot are the security guards and the people who work the ticket counters. A night minister can work best if he/she acknowledges the presence of the security guard and develops a first name familiarity with this person(s). The security guard can indicate people who need special help. One problem in relating to security personnel is that they have very explicit orders about how to handle transients. These orders may be contradictory to the purposes of a night minister. For example, bus depots do not want to become emergency shelters. They will force people to leave the premises if they do not have a current bus ticket. I have seen this policy enforced during very cold weather when elderly women were trying to hide out in the warmth of a bus depot. Security guards are also unlikely to have any training in alcoholism. They can become very abusive when using strong-arm tactics on a drunk. One night in St. Louis I was on duty when a security guard in one of the bus depots became so worked up in a fight with a drunk that he went into cardiac arrest and fell dead on the floor.

When walking through a bus depot late at night I look for people who seem out of place. The shopping bag ladies and other homeless are fairly easy to spot. I will ask if I can be helpful in getting them to a shelter. Sometimes people are taking the bus to get to or in coming from a painful crisis event of some kind. This would include, for example, those going some distance to attend a funeral. There are many different kinds of needs and requests. One night a man pleaded with me to help him get his prescription medicine before his next bus left for a distant state. On another night a young mother with two small children and a baby in diapers was stranded in a bus depot at midnight. She had no friends or family in the city. Her husband "kicked her out" with no money. She did have seven large plastic bags full of clothes for the children. One of the female volunteers was with me at the time of this encounter. The young mother went with the female volunteer to talk about her situation, leaving me and another male volunteer with a crying baby who obviously needed a diaper change. Fortunately, a matronly woman who was watching this scene stepped up and changed the diaper. We did find temporary room for this family in a nearby hotel and gave the mother information for follow-up help.

Waiting Areas Adjacent to Hospital Emergency Rooms

A hospital may or may not be on the turf for a program of downtown late-night ministry. Sometimes these facilities are located at considerable distance from the central downtown core. When they are downtown they become natural settings for ministry. Emergency rooms always have a public waiting area immediately adjacent to the actual clinical areas. This public area is intended for use by family/friends and by people waiting to be admitted for medical help. Large hospitals also become places for transients and others to drop in during the night, especially in cold weather. Security guards are present here as in bus depots to control unwanted transient use and to prevent access to other parts of the hospital.

Social service personnel are conspicuous by their absence in the ER area at night. It is also very unlikely that a chaplain will be present. He or she will normally be "on call" but not physically present unless the hospital is very large or has a program of chaplaincy training with large numbers of interns. When a crisis situation develops and a night minister happens to be on the premises the ER turf can become one of those sacred places for ministry.

There are two ways for a night minister to become involved in the ER area. One is by simply including the hospital on the rounds of places to be visited during a given shift. I always drop by a local hospital at least once during the night. I do not push myself on people. I walk through the waiting area, making my presence known and perhaps stopping to ask someone how they are doing or to say something like "it's a long wait, isn't it?" It is surprising how a simple walk-through can be a lead into major ministry. One of our volunteers, for example, happened to enter the ER area at the same time an ambulance pulled up. This ambulance delivered an elderly woman who had dialed 911 before passing out. She lived alone. She was dead on arrival at the hospital. The night minister was asked to contact family members and to remain to comfort the family. This became an all-night vigil for the clergy person involved.

The other way for a night minister to become involved in the ER setting is to get a telephone call from the nursing staff with a request for a minister. These calls are generally very urgent, demanding immediate response. One night I was asked to help shortly after a middle-aged mother died from injuries in an auto accident. This was a very difficult scene with children, other family members and friends in various stages of profound grief. There were lots of tears. I hugged strangers and cried with them. After three hours of this ordeal I drove home and hugged my wife as I cried some more. Most ER areas have special rooms for grief counseling. ER personnel are very helpful in providing coffee, being attentive to the needs of surviving family members and knowledgeable about such details as the use of a paper bag for deep breathing during the hyperventilation phase of the immediate physical trauma.

As another example of the kind of extreme situations which can be found on the ER turf, I was called one night at the request of a 16-year-old patient. The ER nurses could not get this boy to settle down until they promised to call a minister. He had taken LSD. I rushed to the scene. As I stood by his bed he shared what he described as the most frightful experience of his life. He said that he "nearly died." He talked about fighting to stay alive as his mother sat at his bedside. The "machine" began to falter as a reflection of his irregular heart rhythm. He spoke of being aware of a "white area" around his body. He said that he had "seen Jesus" and that now he had a purpose in life. He wanted to go out and tell other kids to stay away from drugs. His sense of emergency and crisis was exaggerated by the sight of small, white plastic cups stuck to the skin of his bare chest with attached wires leading to monitoring machines. I spent time with this

169

16-year-old, reminding him of the hard, practical decisions after such an emotionally charged encounter.

Ministry of Presence

In downtown ministry a careful analysis of problems such as homelessness and chemical dependency is critical together with a knowledge of available resources. It is also helpful to review the turf, become familiar with taverns, bus depots and sidewalks. But all of this taken together does not produce ministry. The highest priority must be given to the actual work of being the presence of Christ, reaching out in His name to touch others with redemptive love. Without a personal walk with the Lord and sense of commission for ministry a downtown "ministry" becomes just another social program. There are many references to the potential power in simply being available to people as a form of ministry. One of these comes in an editorial titled "Being There" by Rod Brownfield that appeared in *Ministries* in September of 1980. A few lines from this editorial are quoted below:

We always think of Our Lord in terms of the things that he did: he healed, he preached, he taught, he raised the dead, he fed the multitude. True, he did all these things. But we know of these grand deeds because the Gospel is for our instruction, always stressing what God wants of us. But beyond the emphasis on what Jesus did, the remarkable circumstance was his availability. He was always there. He was present to whoever needed him or sought him out, friends and foes alike. We never hear our Lord turning anyone away, even when his disciples urged him to. Martha would reach him to complain of Mary, Nicodemus could find Jesus even in the dead of night. He could turn the wedding at Cana into a grand celebration because he was there. Always and ever, Jesus proclaimed the kingdom of his Father by his very presence, his being available. (Brownfield, 1980, p. 6)

Street Ministry as an Interaction Process

One way to look at street ministry is to imagine a process of interaction. The interaction begins, focuses on primary concerns at the moment and then there is an exit from the interaction. These three basic phases of the process merit careful consideration.

1. Initiation of the Interaction: There must be some way for the exchange to begin. In a church service the beginning is not problematic. A formal order of worship entrenched in the behavioral repertoire of a congregation over the years will guide the exchange between worship leader and others from Sunday to Sunday. But on the downtown streets most encounters between a minister and others are chance meetings of strangers. How does a conversation begin? Can the minister manage the situation in ways which enhance the possibility of a serious exchange?

In most exchanges a rich variety of non-verbal clues are exchanged before any talk ensues. Such factors as tone of voice, facial expression, clothing, rigidity of posture, age and sex are all important. A minister can not simply walk into a strange turf and immediately get into serious dialogue with everyone present. It is important to be sensitive to others, responding to feelings, not just to words while not being repulsed by a barrage of four-letter words. I find that it is sometimes possible to predict the outcome of an exchange based on the nature of the conversation during the initial phase of the process. If a stranger begins by engaging me in a philosophical debate over such issues as creation or the wandering in the wilderness this seldom turns into a sharing of deep spiritual insight. It is a philosophical mindset and very different than the initial exchange in which someone begins by talking about personal pain and loss.

One way to become better in the first phase of interaction is to examine the work of others in street ministry. I have shared many of my encounters in this book. In another book on urban ministry, Mark Van Houten describes an experience in which he was sitting next to a young woman who seemed pre-occupied with her hands. When he looked at her hands he could see that this bothered her. Instead of turning the attention somewhere else he deliberately mentioned her hands during the first few minutes of the exchange. This opened the flood gates of feeling as the stranger freely discussed her use of drugs during which she repeatedly poked needles into her hands leaving visible scars. The young woman was given help toward recovery from drugs, became a Christian and is now helping others. The skillful use of signs and symbols during the initial phase of this contact was critical.

There are a number of pitfalls associated with the first phase of interaction. Sometimes a stranger wants to talk but we read the signals incorrectly and walk away too soon. Other times the first words we hear are so negative and/or abusive that our first inclination is to hurry on to the next place or person. I find that many times a very hostile person changes his/her tone over the period of a contact, becoming very supportive of my presence.

During the early stages of interaction it is all too easy to mistakenly assume that the person in contact does not need or want our help. If this is the way the situation is perceived it will shape the course of the interaction. A classic example of a mismatch between the expectations of one needing help and a professional helper appears in the novel *Madame Bovary*. This 17th century story is about a woman caught in a meaningless marriage who becomes involved in many extra-marital affairs and finally commits suicide. When overcome with feelings of lust for a young man she went to see the village priest. This priest is described in the novel as very busy, trying to control some rowdy boys who were taking classes in catechism. From the story the reader is left to assume that Madame Bovary really wanted to talk with the priest about her lust and her disgust for her husband. She tried again and again to get the priest to consider her needs. But he could not be forced to such a conversation. He simply could not see her as anyone who might ever be in "need." To him she was the wife of his friend, the village physician. He interpreted problems as something the unfortunate folk of the village had, certainly not "Madame Bovary." Her efforts to start a meaningful exchange were thwarted. She walked away and began her course of personal destruction.

2. The Main Phase of the Interaction: If the initial phase goes well the exchange moves on to the actual business at hand. It is in the main phase that serious sharing around problems and solutions develops. It would be very difficult to put a time dimension on these different processes involved in social interaction during street ministry. Sometimes the initiation of action phase passes very quickly into the main phase of interaction. Other times there is a brief greeting and then people go separate ways. But in an ideal situation there is some time for the actual business of the moment. During the main phase the one in contact becomes serious about some issue which merits focused attention.

One important part of main phase action is to determine the nature of the problem. Sometimes keen listening and probing are needed to bring the problem into focus. Sometimes I do this by summarizing the concerns which a person elaborates during his/her talking. Words like "seems to me that you were very depressed at that point" or "you feel that your mother's alcoholism is the major problem now" are natural ways to rephrase and focus the interaction in keeping with the other person's needs.

Other kinds of reactions also come naturally during the main phase of the contact. At some point there will be a consideration of optional lines of action. These may vary from practical activities such as finding shelter for the night to considerations of ways to change attitudes and behavior. Options are best reviewed from within the framework of general information on such basic problems as homelessness, chemical dependency, suicide, mental illness and spiritual need. But there must be an awareness that actual problem situations are never as simple as a listing of problems would suggest. Many times

173

a person on the downtown streets and/or a person in a congregation has many presenting problems. During the main work of a contact it is very important to avoid a purely clinical approach to the person. Ministry is not the same as case work in a social agency or a counseling office. People will not appreciate being scrutinized as if they are applying for some kind of counseling help. At times I have caught myself in the process of pushing my questions too far. For example, when someone starts to share behavior around alcoholism I have on occasion gone on to ask if he has ever had black outs, etc. etc. In my mind at the time I was going over a check-list of the basic characteristics of an alcoholic. If the person senses that one is trying to fit him into a neat clinical category they will resent this. A lot of information can be obtained in a free-flow of feelings without casting the exchange into an obvious attempt to pigeon-hole the other person. One of the main contributions of the street minister is to demonstrate a very deep level of caring. This does not come from a purely clinical approach.

3. Exit From the Interaction: During a contact on the street the minister will start an exchange, continue into the main phase of the interaction and then make an exit. Beginning and ending the exchange are the most problematic parts of the enterprise. As I have indicated, there are many subtle factors involved in determining who will or will not talk to a minister on the downtown streets or in a tavern. There are also a number of important forces at work during the exit from a contact.

For me the contacts with people who are close to a "Skid Road" existence are often easier to end. These people are much more likely to use physical touch during conversations. Sometimes an encounter on the street will begin with an embrace and end with an embrace. A contact in an affluent cocktail lounge is very unlikely to include hugging at any point during the exchange.

In a few situations the minister will want to push for an exit because of feelings that the encounter is turning into a con job or feelings of uneasiness because of a particularly abusive patterns of speech. There are ways to make such an exit. Words like "I must move on to my next contact" or "I am sorry but it is getting late" will generally be understood.

Most of the time the minister will want to terminate the contact in some way which will enhance the value of the interaction that has taken place. This is the time to "tie up loose ends." One way to do this is to use the customer model by simply asking, "what do you wish I could do for you?" This will help tie off the exchange by making sure that problems of real consequence to the person are given attention before exit is completed. It is natural to give the person a card which can be used as a future reference with telephone numbers and the name of the minister in contact. The Northside Ecumenical Night Ministry in Chicago uses a card which gives the telephone number of many agencies.

The referral process merits attention as part of the exit strategy. The best way to make a referral is to give the person the name of someone at the agency or church to which he/she is being referred. Ideally the minister should have some knowledge of intake procedures, the nature of the agency and other details which might be of interest to the one being referred. It is always helpful to give precise directions on how to find the place to which the person is being referred. Sometimes the referral process includes taking the person directly to the place. This is done, for example, when the need is for emergency shelter or detox. If a personal escort is not appropriate or possible during the late evening hours a time can be set up for this kind of contact during the day.

The spiritual power of ministry is important during the exit stage. It is appropriate to say things like "The Lord bless you," and/or to tell someone that you will be praying for them. Sometimes the person will request prayer as part of the process of saying goodbye. When such a request is made it demands an immediate response, a prayer then and there, not at some distant time in the future.

Another part of exiting which must be considered is the issue of how one leaves a situation emotionally when he has been very intensely involved. One does not just walk away with no more thought of those he has touched. It is not always possible to "debrief" with a friend, family member or fellow minister. Sometimes there must be a deliberate attempt to shut off the flow of feelings so that the minister can turn to another problem or get some rest for another day of ministry.

Some General Strategies

At different points in this book I have mentioned general strategies. These strategies can be found in many other programs of urban ministry. Most of them, for example, are given focused attention in Mark E. Van Houten's book which he titles, *God's Inner-City Address* (1988). These strategies are again summarized below:

It is Important to Network with Other Resources

One of the major criticisms of street preachers is that all too often they leave people with words but no concrete help. To give help it is imperative to know community resources. Mark discusses the situation of the woman who says that she has five children, her government assistance has been terminated and her husband has deserted her. Her question is "What the hell am I suppose to do?" A street evangelist might reply "Repent and be baptized." Mark says that this is not the gospel. The gospel is good news, news that God's resources are sufficient. The true minister must know where to turn for help and be willing to take the person to the source of help.

The Minister Must Earn the Right to be on The Turf with Others:

I have implied this in the pages of this book. Mark elaborates on the issue by stating that the minister can not just force his/her way in and be accepted. For Mark, one way to be accepted was to live in the city with the people he served. A street minister earns the right to minister by being available at times of crisis, by showing concern on a regular basis. Once a caring relationship is developed some very strong ties to former strangers are developed.

Personal Safety is an Important Consideration:

Many times people ask me about the danger in being out on the streets of the city late at night alone. I am comfortable in doing this. It is my special commission. But I know that I am making myself vulnerable every night I am out. Mark discusses the role of such factors as prayer, faith and self-awareness. The latter would include a daily, even hourly evaluation of one's strengths and limitations. Street ministry calls for the ability to take inventory of one's physical and emotional state of being. Things like whether one has had enough sleep the night before are important.

There are other practical considerations from a personal safety perspective. It is helpful to know the bartenders, cooks and waitresses on the night turf. The street people are also an important part of the minister's protection system. Being on the street at night demands an awareness of street activity, paying attention to such details as action, movement and mood. When walking along the street at night the minister must show that he/she is aware and alert. "Most victims are people who look like victims." Women in particular need to be careful about what they wear. Sensible clothes which are comfortable and not suggestive are recommended.

The Subtle Attitudes of the Street Minister Can Help or Hurt:

Mark's comments about attitude and behavior merit repeating. As he indicates, the minister must be careful to avoid showing a paternalistic attitude. Such an attitude will not be appreciated by street people or people in a blue-collar tavern. The streets of the city are not the place for a self-righteous attitude. This is also not the place for stereotyping people with labels like "prostitute." The seasoned street minister will prefer to consider the person as a person first, not just someone in a neat category. A judgmental role is not appropriate.

The Street Minister is a Friend and a Shepherd

One key to a ministry of presence is that people in the city are often lonely in spite of the crowds. Mark sees the process of being a friend as central:

In the prophecy of presence, and especially in the mode of a listening prophet, the representation, reminder and messages are about a God who is willing to hear a person out, to dialogue, to interact, to reciprocate and despite the grief this might cause God- to be a friend. (Mark Van Houten, 1988, p. 71)

The minister in the city can be a model of what Christians should be like in responding to personal threats and living by faith. There are times when such a minister must be an advocate. But most of this advocacy will be short-term help kind of advocacy instead of the world-changing variety. Many times people need an advocate to get into a program or to start positive action in some direction. The ministry of presence as described by Mark includes the idea of being a shepherd, watching out for the sheep, taking the words of Psalm 23 seriously:

I am your shepherd; you shall lack nothing.
I make you lie down in green pastures. I lead you beside quiet waters. I restore your soul. I guide you in paths of righteousness for his name's sake. (From Psalms 23:1-3)

Post Traumatic Stress and Street Ministry

Late one night in downtown Denver I met a Vietnam veteran who stood shirtless on the sidewalk. It was a few days before the Fourth of July. When firecrackers exploded near us this veteran cowered against a brick wall. I introduced myself to him as a minister and we talked. He shared the pain of recurring flash-backs to war experiences in Vietnam. At his request I gave him a ride to the V.A. hospital.

During the past several years I have had many occasions to minister to Vietnam Veterans on the streets of different cities as part of my work in late night ministry. Until recently, however, it never occurred to me that there might be a relationship between the kinds of problems facing these veterans and the problems of others whom I see on the streets and in churches where I speak. A generic base for working with major trauma of different types was introduced by Norman Wear, a chaplain at the American Lake Veterans Hospital in Tacoma, Washington, during a workshop I attended. Selected issues as presented by Norm are summarized below. These ideas come both from his own personal experiences in Vietnam and from his intensive work with victims of post-traumatic stress.

An Experience of Major Trauma Upsets Orderly Views of the Nature of God and the World

As reported by Norm, the young men who served in Vietnam were subjected to many disruptions in normal social roles and life expectations. Previous learning experiences clashed with the life-threatening demands of the present. He tells, for instance, of a new soldier who pushed a rifle out of the hands of a buddy when this buddy aimed the rifle at an approaching child. When the gun was knocked aside this young girl continued her walk into a nearby bunker. She was carrying a bomb. The bomb exploded, killing several soldiers. We are brought up with very strong taboos against hurting children. But under the bizarre conditions of war in Vietnam these and other normal kinds of role relationships were turned upside down. Ideas of right and wrong and the role of the Divine were torn from their roots.

Whenever normal expectations and comfort zones are seriously traumatized there are major spiritual consequences. People I see on the street late at night often carry a heavy history of trauma. For some of these folks the early years of life were

179

spent in Sunday School and/or following other formal expectations within the church by adopting the role of an altar boy or the equivalent. Life was moving along a path leading to such standard goals as regular employment and the joys of family life. But some event or combination of events resulted in a mutilation of ordered plans. In the process the experience of simple faith is changed to doubt and confusion. On the street it is the "bad" guys who often seem to win. The drug dealers are kings. There doesn't seem to be much justice in the way some flaunt the laws by persisting in a life of major crime with seeming immunity while others are apprehended and do hard time for petty violations of the law. What is the sense in all of this? Where is God? The world can seem turned upside down from the perspective of the street. Is it possible to look into the face of God after going through the experience of killing another person or the personal violation of being raped or raping another?

It is easy to find examples of the erosion of belief in the face of traumatic events. As street ministers we must be aware of the deep emotional and spiritual wounds which people can receive. A recent publication by Jonathan Kozol titled *Rachel and Her Children* (1988) is a moving account of the plight of homeless children in our country. Kozol interviewed the homeless. He describes an 11-year-old living in a blighted shelter in New York City. When the welfare check for the family did not arrive one day this 11-year-old was caught stealing food from a supermarket. She was brought home in handcuffs. Her mother made the following observation:

> *When I came to this hotel I still believed in God. I said: "maybe God can help us to survive." I lost my faith. My hopes. And everything. Ain't nobody — no God, no Jesus — gonna help us in no way. (Kozol, 1988, p. 67)*

The other night I spent some time talking to a young man as I sat on a bar stool in a tavern. This young man seemed to need to talk to a "man of the cloth" about the trauma in his life. When he was 17, his mother committed suicide. She was a devout member of her church. But the church refused to give her a regular burial because of the suicide. This and other life events resulted in her son leaving the church and searching in desperation for a way to again grasp some handle on faith.

Another way to gain some understanding of the street person is to consider carefully the issue of why someone is caught up in the cycle of the street. This is another way to draw a parallel with the Vietnam experience. According to Norm, most of the young men who served in Vietnam were simply caught up in the net of the draft. They did not enlist. They did not plan life around the glory of one day serving in the military. They were drafted for duty. In many cases these men had high ideals. They did not enroll in college to avoid the draft. They did not turn to wealthy relatives to buy off a draft board. They assumed that when called, one should be loyal to the country. Then when they arrived in the war zone they were hit with the terrible sense of the futility of the whole operation. It became a matter of doing one's time and getting out without being killed. All sense of glory and national honor burned low in the heat of the battle.

One will find different opinions on the issue of why people are on the street. Most of the people I see did not elect to spend life as they are now living it. Like the Vietnam Veteran, they were caught up in a net of circumstances. They too felt that particularly in the United States it is safe to go along with the system. But they quickly moved from a cozy view of life to the harsh realities of the street. Obviously this does not apply to all of those who are on the streets of the city. But many can be understood from the perspective of a trauma model. Unfortunately there are also a number of people in any given congregation who have been seriously traumatized in terms of areas of life most directly related to faith.

Whether in Vietnam or on the streets of one of our major cities, there are people who have encountered evil in a very direct, personal way. War is evil. The struggle for bare survival on the streets of a city day and night can be a very evil experience. Prior to the immersion in evil most people experienced the world as a fairly ordered place. Rules of morality and ethics seemed to make sense, even if they were challenged. But normal rules and any framework of faith can become crippled when evil is confronted. Hostility toward God is one result. In the process there is a loss of innocence.

Remnants of Faith

A linear extension of the above comments would lead to the conclusion that all is lost in terms of spiritual aspirations for either the Vietnam Veteran or the hard core person of the street. This would be an inappropriate conclusion. If we are to minister to people who have been through trauma we must look at how they might view standard symbols of faith. Norm gives the following outline of what is left for those who have been through experiences of deep personal pain:

1. There is a high degree of cynicism about the church. The promises held out by the church are seen as vacuous. Few churches proclaim overtly that a life of faith will result in less pain and more of the good things of life. But this is often the interpretation given by people. With severe trauma the whole business of being rewarded for goodness is seen as just not making sense.

2. The war veteran and the person on the street for a period of time both develop a super-sensitivity to dishonesty. They can detect the false. They know a scam when they see it. Street ministers must be honest in talking about themselves and in the information which they give. The hard core person of the street does not want to be hurt again. This makes him/her reluctant to reach out, even to a clergy person.

3. The survivor of major trauma can best relate to the theology of the cross. He/she may not use this analogy, but this is the best way to interpret such an experience. These people have experienced the suffering of God but they may not know that. They need to be helped to know that the depths of the religious experience come from living the daily life where they are. The combat veteran has been in Hell. He has experienced Jesus with him in a way which is totally alienated from the Sunday School Jesus of his childhood. He has gone far beyond the Jesus of the comfortable after-church coffee hour. But he and the person of the street need help in sorting it all out.

A Personal Encounter With Trauma Always Leaves an After-Taste of Guilt

Both the Vietnam Veteran and the person living on the street easily fall into the pit of feeling soiled, feeling guilty. Street ministers must think through the issue of how to respond to guilt. One frequent manifestation of guilt is reflected in the self-assessment of the middle and late-stage alcoholic. Such a person often refers to himself/herself in very negative terms. I hear a lot of comments to the effect that; "I'm not worth a s . . .," or "I'm not worth a g . . d . . . ." Others on the street will talk about things they have done and express deep feelings of guilt.

In his work with Vietnam veterans, Norman Wear must often manage expressions of guilt. He finds that some men own their guilt while others strike out in anger. This anger may be just a reaction to hidden feelings. The person may not say that he/she is guilty but this may, in fact, be one of the central problems.

As Norm sees the encounter with people who have been through trauma and who carry the trailer of guilt the minister has great potential as a key person to hear the expressions of pain, loss and guilt. Telling the story is a form of confession. By listening we help the person connect their experiences on

183

a feeling level. From my experience in working on the street I now see that at times I have introduced unnecessary hurdles. I am too quick to tell someone that I am not a priest whenever it gets close to confession. People do not need a lot of comments from us. They need to tell their story. We should let them bring up the issue of what kind of priest we are. Our job is to listen, to be there and by our presence and the words we use to extend the forgiveness and love of God.

Another aspect of the guilt situation is the important process of helping the person assume an appropriate level of responsibility. Norm often talks to veterans of the Vietnam war on the issue of who was "at fault." Was the young man guilty or was the entire country guilty for getting involved in the war in the first place? On the street people sometimes take total responsibility for their predicament when in reality many others share in the "guilt." A specific encounter may call for more detailed talking through than we generally get into. The one we are trying to help can better handle guilt if this guilt is placed within an appropriate, specific, personal context. A generalized feeling of guilt for something like the state of our world would be hard to make amends for. I appreciate the work which has been done in reality therapy. On the street we serve best when we help people assume as much responsibility as they are capable of. Defining guilt in a reality framework is part of the process of moving toward individual responsibility. With a direct confrontation of specific patterns of behavior and confession of sin and shortcomings we are better able to become truly whole.

The experience of guilt begs for the process of redemption. Protestantism has a strong tradition around the forgiveness which comes through the freely offered grace of God in the life, death and resurrection of Jesus with little talk of the role of penance. But we each have things which we must do to augment the process of our own redemption and wholeness. Sometimes we can give added power to this process by using the term "penance." Penance is not the same as punishment. Street people will often punish themselves when they are driven by guilt. With experience and sensitivity we can help turn self-punishment in positive directions.

As an example of this process, I am thinking of a man I met one night on Hollywood Boulevard. This stranger pointed to open sores on one hand and complained of swollen hands and feet. His feet hurt so badly that he had removed his shoes to get some relief. When I mentioned medical care he told me that he deserved to suffer because he was not a good person. Among other things he had sold his wedding ring to buy drugs. I spoke of God's love and also reinforced his need to follow through with an appointment at a local drug treatment facility. But I did not link the drug treatment directly to his feelings of guilt and self-hatred. Looking back, I think that I should have mentioned penance openly. I could have said that his penance was to go for treatment. This would be adding pressure to become well, using the guilt in a positive way.

Another side of guilt which I have seen on the street is the deep feeling of guilt about being alive. Sometimes people tell me something like, "everyone in the car was killed, why am I still alive?" This is similar to the question which Norm must respond to when a veteran feels guilty about his own survival when all of his buddies were killed in action. Sometimes survivor guilt is so strong that it occupies all waking hours, leaving little time for daily living concerns. We must help people live **today**.

Pastoral Care Strategy

Most of the above comments are parts of a general strategy for pastoral care. Regardless of the location of contacts there is an ongoing need to evaluate the general strategy of the minister. Street ministry which focuses on people as individuals and not preaching on the sidewalk draws heavily upon the kinds of approaches used by institutional chaplains. It is imperative to be present with people. This means being available and being identified as clergy. "Being there" demands, of course, a psychological as well as a physical presence. It is important to be present even in the face of possible or actual verbal hostility toward any representation of "the church." In ministry it is important to be a catalyst for others to talk. Strangers on the street must be helped to know that it is okay to talk openly with a minister. This openness may take time to develop. It demands a strong feeling that what is told will be handled with confidence. There are very subtle messages which either encourage or discourage a full sharing during interaction on the street.

Very often a one-on-one contact in ministry becomes an opportunity to encourage corporate worship. On the street the experience of group worship might mean participating in a service at a mission or a store front church. Sometimes a large downtown church can be the place for a stranger, even a "street person" to drop in for worship. I am impressed by the number of people on the street at night or in a tavern who talk about praying. We need to encourage a worship/meditation centering. It is all too easy to simply assume that anyone who is poor or marginal in other ways is fit only for talk about sin and salvation.

Burn Out

This book and other writings on downtown ministry can leave the reader with a sense of awe, wonder and romance about the possibility of taking God's call seriously by serving others in today's "urban jungle." With the glamour of street ministry there are also hard realities including stress of different kinds. Whenever ministry includes walking with people in deep crisis it raises the potential for some type of burn-out.

One way to approach stress in street ministry is to distinguish between acute stress episodes and long-term, chronic stress. Acute stress is experienced, for example, when present with family members immediately after a death or when the minister is suddenly in a situation which has the potential for physical harm. This type of stress can have a profound impact on the minister at the time. One of the best ways to manage such stress after the fact is to talk about the crisis event with a significant other. Usually this does not demand in-depth counseling. A friend or spouse can be a very helpful listening resource.

Any form of special ministry working in high crisis environments must allow for the possibility that highly professional help may be necessary after a minister has gone through a particularly draining experience of acute stress. A friend, for example, is a high ranking officer and chaplain in the military. He shared with me the extreme trauma he went through while serving as the chaplain for some 40 men who were dying from a massive fire which erupted in their sleeping quarters. This one episode became such a problem for him that years later he turned to counseling help which used hypnosis to both recapture the horror of the event and lead him into a more positive management of it.

Although the single events can be very difficult it is the steady build up of stress which generates most of the problems labeled under "burn out." Years ago life's major stressful events such a divorce, death and the assumption of a 20 year home mortgage were regarded as reliable predictors of physical and psychological problems. Today there is more focus on the little problems which accumulate and become the basis for major stress.

There is a considerable amount of information about stress. Some of this is helpful when thinking of a particular line of activity such as street ministry. Not all stress is bad. Some is essential to stimulate the normal adaptive capabilities of the body. We have the ability to activate a "relaxation response" as well as a stress response. The bio-feedback movement is successful because of the precise correlation between specific environmental conditions and specific physical events which produce unpleasant sensations including the common migraine headache.

187

The condition which is popularly labeled as burn out is demonstrated in two ways. Both are destructive of effective street ministry. The most obvious form of burn-out is when a street minister (or any minister) must leave his/her position prematurely because of the build up of negative feelings and behavior related to the job. The other type of burn-out is evident when the person remains on the job but becomes so calloused or so worn down by the job that sincere caring and the routine chores of the job are no longer given even the minimum amount of professional attention. People who are burned out but who are still on the job are a major problem in any type of work. Often they have accumulated power in their position over the years. They must change or be replaced but either option may be very difficult to achieve.

The accumulation of stress leading to some form of burn-out invites consideration of the structure of one's daily schedule, the work setting/organization and the combination of factors which resulted in the person getting into ministry in the first place. This calls for an honest review of such simple things as sleep patterns, eating habits, exercise and recreational interests. A separate but very powerful set of factors includes those significant relationships in the family and among friends which become the sociological base for on-going physical and mental health.

Sometimes an amazing change in attitude can follow a sensible re-alignment in the schedule of daily activities. For the minister and for all Christians the daily life of prayer/meditation is also highly significant. I find it essential to both maintain a daily time for spiritual renewal and to have times when I move away from the busy work as part of a period of personal renewal. There is a great source of healing in a conscious practice of becoming open to God during times of personal meditation.

The structure of the organization of the work system is more difficult to understand and/or to manipulate. In street ministry one of my big stressors has been the uncertainty and at times total inadequacy of funding. This has been much more stressful than anything I have experienced on the dark streets at night. This general topic of organizational stress would include such things as the lines of authority, the power coalitions in the organization, relationships with volunteers if any are used and the lines of communication. Street ministry seldom attracts a large-scale organization. This places considerable pressure on the compatibility of those few who are the core members including the board of directors. There must be a very good working relationship between the director and the board or both the director and the program of ministry will show signs of stress.

Why should someone be a street minister? In a recent article Thomas Maeder raises interesting questions in his consideration of "Wounded Healers," (1989). He discusses, for example, "pathological givers." These people may become pastoral counselors and have a degree of success but "they become impoverished after a while." Maeder refers to the work of William Dewart, a clinical psychologist working primarily with clergy persons. This psychiatrist finds that sometimes the clergy are drawn into the profession because of the lure of a position of authority which can compensate for feelings of inadequacy.

In the case of street ministry it is healthy to raise questions about the motivation for involvement. If a person goes out to help as a way to "find himself or herself" this will only create more problems. I respect the standard of many agencies which employ recovering alcohol/drug addicts. This calls for the demonstration of at least two years of personal sobriety before trying to work as a professional counselor. What kind of personal reinforcements does the street minister get? Are there ways in which the very unique work of street ministry makes it even more difficult to look honestly at one's own problems? Perhaps the immediate family of a street minister would be the best place to turn for answers to these questions.

Discussion

It would be difficult to extend the many different lines of inquiry presented in this chapter by giving a few remarks in summary form. I prefer to conclude with two of the bases which I find powerful for me in street ministry.

First it is a source of personal strength to acknowledge that God works with some of the most difficult situations to perform His miracles. Even the most twisted of situations and the weakest of all possible persons can become jewels. For me this means that the person who is down and out and/or a program of ministry which seems to the casual observer to be lacking in power can be transformed by Divine grace. When speaking about street ministry I often give the reading titled *"Touch of the Master's Hand."* The reading was passed on to me from a saintly aunt whose special avocation was the memorizing and giving of such material when she had the opportunity. I share the words below:

The Master's Hand

'Twas battered and scarred, and the auctioneer
Thought it scarcely worth his while
To waste much time on the old violin
But he held it up with a smile.
"What am I offered, good folks, he cried,
Who'll start the bidding for me?"

"A dollar, a dollar, now two only two,
Two dollars and who'll make it three
Going for three. But no.
From the room far back an old gray haired man
Came forward and picked up the bow.
Then wiping the dust from the old violin
and tuning up all the strings,
He played a melody pure and sweet —
As sweet as an angel sings.

The music ceased and the auctioneer
With voice that was quiet and low
Said "What am I bid for the old violin,"

and he held it up with the bow.
"A thousand dollars, who will make it two.
Two thousand dollars who will make it three.
Three thousand dollars once, three thousand
twice and going and gone" He said.
The people cheered but some cried,
"We do not quite understand
What changed its worth?"

A man replied "the touch of the Master's Hand."

And many a man with life out of tune
and battered and torn with sin.
Is auctioned cheap to a thoughtless crowd
Much like the old violin,
A mess of pottage, a glass of wine, a song
and he travels on.
He's going once, and going twice,
He's going and almost gone,
But the Master comes, and the foolish crowd
Never quite understands.
The worth of a soul and the change that is wrought
By the touch of the Master's Hand.

The other touchstone for me is the high ideal for ministry
found in the prayer of Saint Francis of Assisi which I share
below:

Prayer of Saint Francis of Assisi

Lord, make me an instrument of Your peace,
Where there is hatred, let me sow love;
Where there is injury, pardon;
Where there is doubt, faith;
Where there is despair, hope;
Where there is darkness, light;
And where there is sadness, joy.
O divine Master, grant that I may not
So much see to be consoled as to console;
To be understood as to understand;
To be loved as to love;
For it is in giving that we receive;
It is in pardoning that we are pardoned;
And it is in dying
That we are born to eternal life.
                    Amen

191

Additional Information

This is an exciting time for ministry. There is growing interest in such issues as environmental pollution and the kinds of problems mentioned in this book. It is a good climate for the serious exploration of a wide variety of topics. Serving others in ministry now more than ever calls for a fresh look at problems from different perspectives. The pages in this part of the book should serve to complement other exposures to alcoholism, drug addiction, suicide and mental illness. Coupled with a strong background in Biblical studies and Theology this type of material can enrich the process of reaching out to touch people in His name.

Chapter 8
Alcoholism

If one is facing a personal problem with alcohol abuse involving himself or a family member or friend one natural response will be to pray about the problem. Prayer is important. But prayer should not be used as a way to avoid problems associated with alcohol abuse. The attitude should not be that everything is to be simply put in God's hands with nothing for us to do. Many alcoholics have died while a spouse or friend prayed for them but continued to enable them to drink by doing things like covering up for them and giving them money to drink on. In Alcoholics Anonymous the Serenity Prayer is encouraged; "God grant me the serenity to accept the things I cannot change, courage to change the things I can, and wisdom to know the difference." This prayer is good for the spouse of the alcoholic as well. Another way to pray is to consider prayer as a form of daily meditation. The specific words are not as significant as the attitude of deliberately placing oneself in God's presence at the beginning of the day. Some prayers can be prayers for strength to follow through on a hard decision around the personal use of alcohol or appropriate behavior to get an alcoholic into treatment.

Who is An Alcoholic?

As a starting point in a discussion of who is an alcoholic it is imperative to make a distinction between drinking, being drunk and alcoholism. This may seem elementary but it is important. When applied to alcohol use drinking refers to the practice of consuming beverage alcohol or ethanol. Since recovered alcoholics continue to refer to themselves as alcoholic it is possible to be an alcoholic without drinking in the present tense. It is also generally the case that people drink without

193

getting drunk or becoming alcoholic. The consumption of alcohol in some form such as in beer, wine or whiskey is widespread in most cultures.

Ministers who become involved in a street/tavern ministry are often surprised by the drinking patterns which they encounter. In a downtown tavern some patrons sit throughout the evening while consuming very little alcohol. These people may order a beer and then hold the glass for a long period of time. Sometimes they get up from the bar and leave a half-filled glass. For these people the tavern is a place to go for social contact. On the other hand, some tavern patrons are very drunk before they attempt to order a drink in a tavern. These people and others who are not so drunk at first come primarily to drink as much as they can pay for. Others on the downtown scene can be seen at any time of the day or night passing a common bottle of cheap wine from mouth to mouth as they stand or sit with buddies on the sidewalk.

The term "drunk" refers to temporary loss of control from the drinking of alcohol. In contrast to the considerable amount of disagreement over the appropriateness of drinking there is general agreement that being drunk is not a desirable condition. Someone is regarded as being drunk when his/her sensory and motor systems are noticeably impaired together with signs that drinking has occurred. Anyone who staggers when walking or who weaves in and out of a traffic lane while driving is generally seen as being drunk. The label can be misleading, however, since a number of health problems can produce the same behavioral effects as an over-indulgence in beverage alcohol. One problem for the street minister is to be alert to a range of possibilities when meeting a person who seems to be having considerable problems with psycho-motor control.

An understanding of the experience of being drunk demands an awareness of the effects of alcohol upon the body. Concentrations of alcohol in the body are usually measured in terms of blood alcohol level (BAL) or blood alcohol content (BAC). These levels are normally determined by extrapolating from the alcohol levels in alveolar air drawn from the lungs during a breathalyzer test. The legal level for being drunk (driving while under the influence of alcohol) is 0.10 in most states. This means that being drunk in terms of ability to drive a car is achieved when there is only one tenth of one percent alcohol in the blood.

There are many factors that produce the condition of being drunk. The most important of these factors are the amount of alcohol which is ingested and the rate of ingestion. When alcohol and its by-products begin to accumulate in the body intoxication will occur. Although alcohol is readily absorbed into the blood stream it must be broken down or converted to other substances to continue its passage through the system. The metabolism of alcohol occurs at a rate which allows for the ingestion of from one third to one half ounce of absolute alcohol per hour for a person who weighs 150 pounds and who does not have liver damage (an ounce of 100 proof whiskey is one half ounce of absolute alcohol.) It is the alcohol content of a drink which becomes important, not the type of drink that is consumed. There is actually more alcohol in a 12 ounce bottle of four percent beer (.48 ounce of absolute alcohol) than there is in one ounce of 86 proof liquor (.43 ounce of absolute alcohol). This does not mean that a person can sit and drink one beer an hour for hours on end without feeling any ill side effects. It simply means that under the best conditions the body should be able to metabolize an occasional drink over a reasonable time period without showing signs of being intoxicated.

There are dangers in equating the state of drunkenness with the amount of alcohol consumed and also major problems in using drunkenness as a symptom of alcoholism. Over time people develop a tolerance for alcohol. This means that they must drink larger amounts to get the same effect. Increasing tolerance is one of the danger signs of alcoholism. The alcoholic reaches the point where he/she appears to be under control when in fact he/she has consumed considerable amounts of alcohol. This is most obvious in the population of Skid Road alcoholics processed through a public detox center. Most text book material suggests that a person will experience a coma or will be unconscious with a blood alcohol content (BAC) of 0.40 percent and be dead at a level in excess of something like 0.50 percent. But I have seen detox reports that regularly list BAC levels in excess of 0.48 percent or almost five times the legal "drunk" level. There are cases on record where BAC levels have exceeded 0.70 percent and even 0.85 percent.

The condition of being drunk may or may not be part of the pattern of alcoholism. Obviously a person may get drunk as a once in a life time affair or as part of a very rare drinking episode. Such drunkenness should not be confused with the disease of alcoholism. There are alcoholics who are maintenance drinkers. These are drinkers who become complusive about regular intake of alcohol but who do not drink to the point of being drunk. Although these people never get drunk they are alcoholic and will show all the physical, psychological, sociological and spiritual deterioration which comes from the disease. With sufficient money an alcoholic who gets drunk can hide this drunkenness by getting away from family and friends. A wealthy woman living on the West Coast, for example, made regular weekend trips to Hawaii where she became very, very drunk far away from the prying eyes of her neighbors. Some people, including housewives, can control their most obvious signs of intoxication by planning their drinking around times when they do not expect family members to be present. These patterns sometimes serve to hide the real problem until considerable damage to the person has occurred.

The Uniform Alcoholism Act for the State of Washington contains the following definition:

> *"Alcoholic" means a person who habitually lacks self-control as to the use of alcoholic beverages or uses alcoholic beverages to the extent that his health is substantially impaired or his social or economic function is substantially disrupted.*

196

Before a major disruption in life occurs because of drinking some early warning signs can be noted. A number of different lists of such signs are readily available from sources like AA and community mental health centers. The following is one of the most popular of these lists.

A Test to Indicate Possible Alcoholism:

1. Do you occasionally drink after a disappointment or quarrel?

2. Do you drink more than usual when you're under pressure or feel troubled?

3. Are you able to handle more liquor than you could when you first started drinking?

4. The morning after you have been drinking, do you forget what you said the night before or how you got to bed?

5. When you drink, do you have a few extra when others will not know it?

6. Are there occasions when you feel uncomfortable if alcohol isn't available?

7. Have you noticed that you're in more of a hurry to get the first drink than you used to be?

8. Do you sometimes feel guilty about your drinking?

Some professionals prefer more general signs that point to problems such as; 1. A growing sense of looking foward to the next drink, 2. Rigidity in drinking behavior (for example, the felt necessity to drink at the same specific time every day). and 3. A growing tolerance for alcohol. One of the major problems in the application of any list of signs or symptoms is that the alcoholic is caught up in a web of denial. The non-alcoholic can look at a list and very likely draw the intended conclusions. But the interpretation may become very clouded within a denial framework.

Another way to talk about the differences between alcoholics and non-alcoholics is to point to physical differences. There are physical differences between alcoholics and non-alcoholics that are reflected in the way alcohol is processed through the body. The importance of basic physical differences is supported by research that shows a greater prevalence of alcoholism among relatives of alcoholics. Experimental data is now being accumulated on differences in the metabolic conversion of alcohol by the body. One important step in this metabolism is the production of acetaldehyde as a by-product. In the future it may be possible to give tests that detect a physical propensity for alcoholism before anyone begins a drinking career.

The behavioral signs which accompany alcoholism are most likely to be noticed first by someone other than the alcoholic. Some of these signs are directly related to the behavior around drinking such as the practice of sneaking drinks and drinking to get ready to attend an affair where more drinking will be taking place. Other behavioral signs including a tendency to pull away from people and making up excuses for drinking are more subtle. In the identification of alcoholism serious consideration must be given to the person as a whole.

The "alcoholic syndrome" includes feelings of omnipotence and low frustration tolerance. Feelings about self fluctuate from extreme inferiority feelings to grandiosity. In the same sentence an alcoholic may proclaim that he/she is worth nothing and then that he/she has a grand scheme to solve all of the world's problems. It is hard for the alcoholic to empathize with other people. He/she is also likely to have problems because of patterns of perfectionism or idealism. This may be reflected in such behavior as constantly riding others for their faults while not performing adequately himself/herself. These behaviors point to confusion and stress. Most people have occasions when they feel this way but the alcoholic is different in that he/she turns to alcohol as a major way to cope with stressful situations.

The alcoholic increasingly withdraws from others and from realistic feedback about his/her condition. Counselors see this as a formidable wall which must be penetrated to get through to the hurting person. The feelings of disgust for self are dramatically displayed in late stage alcoholism. On a recent ride in a detox van I watched as a Skid Road wino was picked up. He mumbled to himself in the back of the van as he tried to maintain a sitting position. The driver of the van told me that this derelict had just been released from detox only the day before. In his mumbling I picked up parts of sentences. Most of the words were words of self condemnation . . . "I ain't worth a s . . ., I ain't worth a g . . d . . ."

The pattern of attitudes and behaviors that make up the alcoholic syndrome is sometimes used when counseling a recovered alcoholic as warning signs which may point to a possible relapse. The alcoholic may show marked tendencies to fluctuate from inferiority feelings to grandiosity and low frustration tolerance before lapsing into another drinking episode. One of the functions of peer group support in organizations like AA is the provision of feedback from others and the opportunity to freely express frustrations.

As suggested above, sometimes it is helpful to be aware that there are different types of alcoholics. The most popular list of types was suggested by E.M. Jellineck in 1960. Some people have a psychological dependence on alcohol. Jellineck referred to these people as "Alpha type" alcoholics. Although they do not have a physical addiction, show little or no progression and no withdrawal symptoms they can present a major problem for other family members and work associates because of their drinking. These people use alcohol to boost morale, block out reality, bolster self-confidence or to relieve emotional or bodily pain.

Another type of alcoholic is Jellineck's "Beta" type, the person whose excessive drinking is related to a social dependency on alcohol. Such a person may manifest a number of problems associated with excessive drinking including nutritional deficiencies as well as organic damage such as cirrhosis of the liver and gastritis. The drinking for this type of alcoholic is largely socio-cultural or situational. It is more common in occupations where "everybody" gets drunk on the weekend.

The third type described by Jellineck, the "Gamma" type is what people generally think of when they refer to alcoholism. The Gamma type demonstrates all of the symptoms of chronic, progressive alcoholism. Psychological dependency progresses to physical dependency. There is a progressive loss of control over how much one drinks. The late stage Gamma type is often seen staggering along the downtown streets of any large city.

The final two types in the work of Jellineck are not as visible on the city streets but are found in many social and work settings in our society. The "Delta" type is made up of people who are maintenance drinkers. They must have a regular input of alcohol. Although they may never get drunk they consume so much alcohol on a regular basis that they go into severe withdrawal if deprived suddenly for some reason. It is the Delta type alcoholic who sips drinks from a hidden supply throughout the work day. Several years ago when working for the State of Washington a colleague of mine was a good example of this type of alcoholic. She drank throughout the day but was never "staggering" drunk. In her job she served as the liaison person for the agency, a critical public relations position!

The "Epsilon" type described by Jellineck is more hidden than any other type of alcoholic. This is the binge drinker. Such an alcoholic can abstain for long periods. But once he/she starts drinking heavily the drinking may continue until a stuporous condition is achieved. In some cases periods of abstinence may last as long as a year. A few years ago a nationally respected corporate executive died while on vacation. It was only after his death that friends and family members recognized the fatal trail of drunken binges which always accompanied his annual vacations. Death came during one of these drinking episodes. Most of his business associates would never have labeled him as an alcoholic. He was a binge drinker, one of the "Epsilon" types who would perhaps be alive today if someone could have penetrated the facade of his alcoholic lifestyle.

Since alcoholism is a progressive illness the signs of its progression can be used as indicators of the disease. Purely "social" drinkers differ from alcoholics both in how much they drink and the reasons for their drinking. The alcoholic passes a line where the two drinks a day as part of a social group become an increasingly larger number of drinks consumed primarily for the effect. Eventually the alcoholic drinks because he/she is most comfortable when drinking. It becomes less painful to drink than not to drink. A number of social, physical and psychological changes accompany the progressive debilitation of the alcoholic.

The Glatt model for the progression of alcoholism is a standard reference. This chart appears in modified form together with explanatory comments in the 1981 publication of *James Royce* (pp. 98-99). One important early sign shown on the Glatt chart and in many other contexts is an increase in tolerance for alcohol. This is followed by such reactions as; increasing dependence on alcohol, concerns/complaints of family, feelings of guilt, alibis for drinking, hiding bottles, attempted geographical escape, avoidance of family and friends, neglect of food and ethical deterioration.

One advantage in thinking of progression and alcoholism is that it is possible to consider stages in recovery as well as the stages leading down into alcoholism. It is not necessary for an alcoholic to reach the stage of near total destruction before climbing back through the process of recovery. Surrender and total abstinence can occur at any point. Turning to the Glatt chart again, some of the key points along the road to recovery are; stop taking alcohol, meeting happy, sober alcoholics, guilt reduction, onset of new hope, adjustment of family needs, rebirth of ideals and steps toward economic stability.

A final way to gain perspective on alcoholism is to emphasize what alcoholism is not. One major problem in the reactions to the alcoholic is that he/she is often identified as having everything from arthritis to psychosis when the problem is really alcoholism. A middle-class woman who takes her symptoms to her family physician is probably more likely to be given minor tranquilizers which only exacerbate her problem than to be told in a straight-forward way that she is showing symptoms of alcoholism. The psychiatrist may label an alcoholic as manic-depressive. The minister or priest may focus entirely on salvation. Friends may consider loss of energy and irregular work habits as problems of poor nutrition. The alcoholic may in fact have all of these problems plus many more. But the myriad problems must be placed appropriately within the context of the disease of alcoholism.

In the past the focus on the uniqueness of this disease became dysfunctional by creating a cult-like atmosphere among alcoholism professionals. Some agencies have made it a practice, for example, not to hire anyone who is not a recovered alcoholic. The rationale for this is that the experience of being an alcoholic is a very peculiar experience, one which an "outsider" could never understand. Alcoholism is the prototype of the diseases that impact the whole body. This means that a wide range of disciplines and professionals can and should have input into the healing process. The most promising work in alcoholism and drug addiction in general is now in the arena of interdisciplinary studies and applications. New knowledge of the brain is only one of the factors promoting this new frontier. Professionals now working in this field must become more open to models of intervention that hold the promise of improved rates of recovery, especially for the late-stage alcoholic.

Alcohol and the Body

Alcohol is not digested like coffee, tea or milk. It is formed of molecules small enough to be absorbed directly into the blood stream. The circulatory system carries the alcohol to every cell in the body. But first it must be released from the digestive system into the circulatory system. Alcohol goes from the mouth through the esophagus to the stomach. In normal social drinking the esophagus simply transports the alcohol like any ingested material. With chronic alcoholism, however, a number of disorders of the esophagus can occur. These disorders range from inflammation to severe laceration and rupture.

When alcohol enters a stomach that contains partly digested food from recent eating the alcohol will be slowed down in its passage through the body. The main reason for this is that most of the alcohol is absorbed into the blood stream from the small intestine, not the stomach. Alcohol is absorbed in very small amounts through the lining of the mouth and the esophagus, more through the stomach and 70 percent to 80 percent through the upper or small intestine. To complete the process of absorption, therefore, the alcohol must get out of the stomach so that it can be fully introduced into the circulatory system. When the stomach contains food, a muscle called the pylorus contracts to hold the food so that normal digestion can occur. The alcohol is held in the stomach along with the food. This control of the flow of stomach content into the small intestine is an important process for normal digestion. The small intestine is a series of coiled tubes located directly beneath the stomach. Although held in a compact area, this portion of the intestine is actually about 22 feet long. Most of the alcohol that is taken into the body is absorbed by the circulatory system in the first foot long section of the small intestine called the duodenum. Only about five percent of the ingested alcohol escapes from the body in exhaled air, perspiration or urine. Some 95 percent must be converted in some way and managed within the body.

The liver is the most important clearing house for ingested alcohol. All of the circulating blood passes through this large body organ which is located in the front upper right part of the body. Since alcohol is a foreign substance it must be converted in some way to be handled by the body. It is ultimately converted to carbon dioxide (CO_2), water and energy. Most of the important chemical transformations occur in the liver.

The first step is the transformation to a substance called acetaldehyde. Since acetaldehyde is a toxic substance it must also be transformed. It is converted to acetic acid through the action of various chemicals. The acetic acid is then transformed to carbon dioxide, water and energy. One common form of treatment includes the use of a substance called Antabuse (Disulfiram). When Antabuse is taken, the alcoholic will have severe painful reactions if he/she should drink. These reactions, or the fear of them, reinforce abstinence. Antabuse works by blocking the conversion of acetaldehyde. This produces a build up of the toxic substance. Antabuse should be administered only under medical supervision. Another important feature of the metabolism of alcohol is that over time the cells of the liver can be totally destroyed as they are required to over-work in handling alcohol and its by-products. Death from cirrhosis of the liver is one of the real possibilities for the late-stage alcoholic.

Alcohol and the Brain

Ingested alcohol very quickly reaches the brain. This is demonstrated by the sudden changes in behavior that can be observed in the naive drinker after only one or two drinks on an empty stomach. Since alcohol is transported by the blood to all cells of the body those cells most richly innervated by blood vessels are the first to be affected by drinking. The brain has a very dense supply of arteries and veins in comparison to areas of large, smooth muscle, for example.

Making it to the brain is like making it to the inner workings of a vast computer for a large corporation. The brain monitors and controls all body processes. The most critical activity of the brain and other parts of the nervous system involves the functioning of specialized nerve cells called neurons. Normal thinking and behavior depend upon the ability of neurons to convey impulses and thus to communicate with other neurons. When one touches his finger on a hot stove, for example, a sensory message is sent from the finger tip up the arm and into the spinal cord to trigger a reflexive withdrawal of the hand from the stove. This occurs without conscious thinking but it does involve a nervous system pathway where nerve cells communicate with each other. A considerable range of possibilities for communication exists because of the way neurons are linked to each other. They do not connect directly. Impulses must pass across a microscopic distance between neurons through the activity of chemical substances called neurotransmitters. This allows for considerable variability in behavior but also poses major problems when neurotransmitter activity is impaired by alcohol or some other drug or from hereditary abnormalities as part of dysfunctions such as schizophrenia.

Alcohol has a generalized effect upon brain function by directly impacting neuronal activity or indirectly as it modifies the critical life support system of the brain, the blood supply. Alcohol also has selective influence on specific parts of the brain. Lower areas of the brain control such life sustaining functions as breathing and heart beat. Other parts of the brain control and monitor the motor movements involved in such activities as walking and speaking. Higher areas of the brain sustain the functions needed for long-term memory and critical thinking. Abnormal behaviors of a specific type while intoxicated are the result of the selective influence of alcohol on specific parts of the brain.

It is common to refer to the sedative effects of alcohol upon the brain. Alcohol is one of the sedative-hypnotic drugs. But the first effects of alcohol are in the form of an irritation to the nervous system. This produces a form of stimulation that occurs prior to the sedative effect. On a long-term basis as part of a pattern of alcoholism, alcohol will irritate, sedate and finally kill neurons.

When discussing the effects of alcohol upon neurons it is important to consider both acute or temporary and chronic or long-term effects. Low doses of alcohol have the immediate effect of making cell membranes less fluid, for example. Moderate to high doses result in the cell membrane becoming more fluid while very high doses dissolve the membrane producing cell death. One of the chronic effects of over-consumption is that cell membranes can become toughened to the point where some alcohol is needed for the cell to function in a near-normal way. This becomes one of the characteristics of a physical addiction to alcohol. The person actually performs somewhat better when alcohol is available to the nervous system. This alcohol is, however, producing more damage to the system.

Most of the problems for the brain from an over-consumption of alcohol occur because specific requirements for nerve cell functioning are jeopardized. In addition to damage to structures of the cells there are deficiencies in important elements such as oxygen, glucose and thiamine (Vitamin B_1). Since glucose and oxygen are carried to the brain by the blood stream any serious impairment of normal circulation will reduce the brain's supply of these life-sustaining materials. There are many ways in which chronic alcoholism impairs the circulation of blood. Alcohol reduces the efficiency of the heart, it causes a "sludging" of blood cells which interferes with circulation and produces brain cell death which also impairs circulation. The extensive over-consumption of alcohol can also modify the basic processes that surround the production and availability of essential neurotransmitters.

One of the many types of brain damage that is most closely asociated with the effects of alcohol is the condition known as alcoholic dementia. This is sometimes seen in the late stages of alcoholism. The symptoms are usually very slow in becoming apparent. These symptoms include: impairment of reasoning, deterioration of memory, fatigue, depression and social withdrawal. If alcoholic dementia is untreated it can progress to a bedridden state and even to death. The condition represents an atrophy or premature aging of the brain. Treatment includes total abstinence and good health care. If this treatment is started early some gradual restoration of brain function can occur.

One of the most often mentioned forms of brain damage due to malnutrition from alcoholism is the Wernicke-Korsakoff Syndrome. The symptoms of this disorder are: muscular incoordination, paralysis of eye movements, hypothermia, memory loss and confabulation. The latter condition is an attempt on the part of the person to compensate for memory loss by filling in the gaps with bits of information in an attempt to cover up for a total lack of ability to recall what happened during a given period of time. The primary cause of Wernicke-Korsakoff Syndrome is deficiency of thiamine (Vitamin B_1). Treatment includes immediate administration of thiamine, abstinence from alcohol and vitamin supplements. It is a general practice to routinely give thiamine injections to incoming patients at a public detox facility. Early treatment can produce remarkable recovery in a short time. Permanent disability and death are possible if treatment is delayed.

Psychosocial and Spiritual Aspects of Alcoholism

The discussion of who is an alcoholic included many references to the complexity of the disease. As indicated, the physical aspects of alcoholism are only one part of the problem. Alcoholics develop serious maladjustments in psychological, sociological and spiritual functioning. It is therefore misleading to refer to alcohol abuse as simply a physical addiction. A total lifestyle sustains the abuse. One manifestation of this lifestyle is the increasing inability to really see what is happening in relation to the drinking.

Normally when we engage in behavior that has negative consequences we use the feedback to modify future behavior. For example, if one should trip on a rug while crossing the floor in his home, fall, and in the process break an expensive, crystal glass he would most likely either detour around the rug in the future or smooth it out to avoid tripping again. If someone goes through this experience but then talks about how much he enjoyed the sense of freedom during the few seconds when he was falling and goes on to say that the crystal glass really needed to be broken we would question the person's sanity. But this is the kind of irrational thinking the alcoholic engages in. He/she loses the normal ability to use consequences to modify future behavior when that behavior is related in some way to drinking. Such thinking reinforces the potential value of either a crisis event or the work of a professional counselor to push the kind of break-through needed for recovery to begin.

The profile of the alcoholic as given in this section may seem overly depressing. Is it possible for an alcoholic to change? The host of people now attending AA meetings regularly represent only one of the very visible reminders that recovery is possible.

Street ministers with some background in alcoholism are one of the most valuable community resources for the disease. Few professionals dare to walk openly with people who are in some stage of inebriation. The street minister must touch people where they are. Much of the work which I report has been done within the setting of the tavern. I have seen alcoholics literally cry for help. Not all will recover. I have talked to a few shortly before their death. Sincere ministry does not turn away from the alcoholic at any stage. When others shout "leper" the street minister goes quietly about his or her work reaching out in small and major ways.

Summary

Alcoholism is a disease to be understood as something not necessarily charactertized by drunkenness. Many "tests" are available, pointing to possible alcoholism. Generally they suggest such factors as frequency of and reasons for drinking.

A considerable body of literature is now available on alcoholism. This includes discussions of various types of alcoholics as in the work of Jellineck and considerations of the progression of the disease. Ministers and other professionals must avoid being mislead by the tendency to see the symptoms of alcoholism as something other than this disease.

Research is now generating more helpful information on how the body, including the brain, manages the foreign substance of beverage alcohol. The liver is the primary organ for the metabolism process. The brain is both one of the first body systems to feel the impact of ingested alcohol and one of the systems seriously insulted in cases of chronic alcoholism.

Alcoholism affects body, brain, and total life style. The cumulative effects can make recovery difficult. But testimony at AA meetings, the results of street ministries like Operation Nightwatch and other forms of intervention all point to the possibility of major transformation for the alcoholic.

Chapter 9

Drug Addiction

The last chapter included a brief reference to the way alcohol affects the brain. One of the most important images to keep in mind with respect to drugs other than alcohol is that they have the potential for a powerful, direct effect on brain functioning.

This effect is possible because of the basic design of the brain. As suggested in the last chapter, all behavior and thought processes depend upon an electrical-chemical system linking one neuron to another. It is the chemical part of this system which is directly impacted by the introduction of drugs. Normal neuronal activity includes the release of chemical substances called neurotransmitters across a microscopic space between neurons which is called the synapse. A message arrives at a synapse and then there is first a release of a neurotransmitter and then a re-uptake of the neurotransmitter after the message crosses the synapse. When there is an artificial distortion in the normal chemical processes this can have temporary or long-term effects depending on the amount and duration of drugs taken.

The tremor of Parkinson's disease is a vivid example of how distortions in brain chemistry can affect the body. In the special case of this disease, the neurotransmitter dopamine (DA) is not able to function normally. A few years ago one clinic in California reported a strange increase in the number of 20-30-year-olds showing the symptoms of Parkinson's. The mystery was solved when it was discovered that these patients had all used a specific illicit drug extensively prior to the onset of the symptoms. Cocaine or heroin do not produce Parkinson's disease. But extended use will result in a number of abnormal signs and symptoms. Recent years have seen a remarkable increase in the number of admissions to mental hospitals of people who have no history of psychosis but who do have extensive experience with drugs of different kinds.

Different Kinds of Drugs

There are many sources of information on different kinds of drugs for inclusion in a review of "drug abuse." One thing to keep in mind is that these drugs are illegal or tightly controlled. This places them in a very different category than alcohol, a socially accepted drug. Simply having a small amount of an illegal drug can result in arrest and time in jail. In one way, therefore, drugs are a problem no matter how much they are used by the person. Serving time in jail can result in a major disruption of life. The possession of drugs is also much more likely to mean the presence of a problem than the possession of a bottle of wine because the drug possession means that the person is in a social network that includes drug transactions. This illegal network is very hard to confront because it is illegal.

Looking at different kinds of drugs it is also important to note that the common practice is for people to be poly-drug abusers. They use many different kinds of drugs. This often includes alcohol. A person can get high on one drug and use another to "come down" on, for example. The effects of a drug will also vary from one individual to another. I have seen marked paranoid delusions from cocaine use, for example, one particular symptom not present in everyone.

Another interesting observation as one reads through the following list of general categories of drugs is that many drugs have both common and medical uses which are highly valued. This list is not intended to cover the array of drugs one may encounter when trying to intervene with someone who is addicted. An important category not included, for example, is the so-called "designer drugs," both very powerful and very dangerous. On the street I have seen the impact of some very strange combinations including an episode on Denver's streets

211

at night when a woman stood in front of me spraying a can of paint thinner into a tissue and then pushing this up her nose.

Narcotics

This term is often mistakenly used with reference to the entire drug scene. Its use is most properly restricted to only opium and drugs derived from opium or synthetic products that simulate these drugs. The narcotics are used extensively in medical practice to relieve pain. They are also used in such common medications as cough suppressants. The best known of the narcotics are opium, morphine, heroin, codeine and methadone.

One of the dangers of narcotic addiction is that the addict reaches the point where near lethal doses are required to obtain the desired effects. Repeated use results in increasing tolerance as larger doses are needed for the same effect. But the amount that will result in an overdose does not change. Addicts often become pre-occupied with the procuring and taking of drugs. In the process they often neglect themselves and may suffer malnutrition, infections and unattended diseases or injuries. In the case of narcotics and other addictive drugs there is an alteration in the normal functioning of the body which demands the drug to prevent withdrawal effects. These effects are most intense during the 72 hour period immediately after the last dose has been taken. One treatment alternative is to administer methadone as a substitute for the illegal narcotic and then to gradually reduce the methadone dosage. Total treatment must include a drastic alteration of lifestyle to encourage drug-free living.

Depressants

This group of drugs is potentially dangerous for the alcoholic because a cross-tolerance is developed for them in the process of becoming an alcoholic. Another feature of the depressants is that they are readily available and widely used. They are routinely prescribed by physicians for the relief of such common ailments as insomnia, anxiety, irritability and tension. In excessive amounts, however, they produce a state of intoxication that is remarkably similar to that of alcohol. Intoxicating doses invariably result in impaired judgment, slurred speech and loss of motor coordination. Such conditions as drowsiness, sleeplessness, stupor and coma and even death can result. The most popular of the depressants are alcohol, anesthetics, barbiturates, sleeping pills and tranquilizers.

The abusive patterns in the case of the depressants very considerably. Sometimes there is a temporary, rare incident of abuse when a teen-ager experiments with the contents of the family medicine cabinet or responds to peer pressure. Those who experience increasing dependence upon any of the depressants can suffer the total range of physical, social and emotional debilitation. The withdrawal experience is more severe in the case of depressants than in a comparable case of narcotic addiction. One of the forms of abuse includes the deliberate intake of a depressant drug as a means of suicide.

Stimulants

The stimulants are chemicals that stimulate the brain. It is not unusual for people to turn to different resources including chemicals as a means to enhance feelings of well-being. The temporary elevation in mood must be balanced against the long-range effects in the case of any nervous system stimulant. The most popularly used stimulants are nicotine as contained in tobacco products and caffeine, the active ingredient in coffee, tea and most popular soft drinks. Other stimulants are amphetamines, speed, cocaine, preludin and ritalin.

A variety of sensations are possible with the injection of stimulants. States of high exhilaration and superabundant energy are reported. But irritability, anxiety and apprehension

213

are also possible. One of the major problems is the depression which follows after the stimulation wears off. These unpleasant episodes can be avoided with additional injections of the stimulant. Heavy users may inject themselves every few hours, a process sometimes continued to the point of delirium, psychosis or physical exhaustion. It is not clear that physical dependence is developed in the case of stimulants. But strong psychological dependence does develop. Anxiety, an incapacitating tenseness and suicidal tendencies may persist for weeks or months after a chronic pattern of use is terminated.

Hallucinogens

In contrast to many of the other types of drugs, medical science has found little use for any of the hallucinogenic substances. The hallucinogenic trip became popular in the 1960s when young people turned on with LSD. The effects of LSD were first demonstrated by a chemist in 1943. He accidentally took some LSD and went on a two hour trip which included feelings of restlessness and bizarre visions. The hallucinogenic drugs are substances which distort the perception of objective reality. They produce sensory illusions making it difficult to distinguish between fact and fantasy. In addition to LSD which is produced from a natural substance found in a fungus of rye the hallucinogens include peyote and mescaline from one of the ingredients of the peyote cactus and PCP, a synthetic product first developed in the 1950s.

The greatest hazard of the hallucinogens is that their effects are unpredictable each time they are taken. Toxic reactions that precipitate psychotic reactons and even death can occur. Persons in hallucinogenic states should be closely supervised and upset as little as possible to keep them from harming themselves and others. There is no documented withdrawal syndrome. The hallucinogens have therefore not been shown to produce physical dependence.

Cannabis

This drug is more popularly known as marijuana or the more potent hashish. The legal reactions to marijuana use have varied considerably over the last several years and vary from state to state within the United States. The marijuana plant has many uses. It is grown illegally in California and many other states today but historically it was grown almost exclusively in Jamaica, Columbia, Mexico, Africa, India and the Middle East. The effects of marijuana can be interpreted in terms of the amount of the drug introduced into the body. With low doses the following effects have been noted: feelings of restlessness, increased sense of well being, alternation of sensory perceptions and subtle changes in thought formation and experiences. Moderate doses can produce such effects as rapidly changing emotions, dulling of attention, impaired memory and an altered sense of self-identity. High doses can result in distortions of body image, loss of personal identity, fantasies and hallucinations. Very high doses may precipitate a toxic psychosis.

Marijuana has been associated with dependence patterns. Withdrawal problems have been reported. These include sleep loss and disturbance, irritability, restlessness, hyperactivity and decreased appetite. These problems are evident primarily in cases of extreme heavy use of this drug.

Discussion

This book is about touching lepers. Drug addicts are some of the most marked lepers in our society today. I struggle with them as they reach for some small sign of hope and health. A few nights ago I saw a heroin addict on the street late at night in the rain. She gave me some money to send to her husband who is in jail. I hugged her, telling her that I loved her. I have seen her many times. On this night as I held her in the rain she grabbed my raincoat and held on like a small

215

child. She was hurting. She wants so much to live a normal life. But she knows and I know that there are many obstacles to this. It is the pull of the individual addict that really gets to me.

The additional information on drugs in the above pages gives an over-view of key drug groups including narcotics, depressants, stimulates and hallucinogens.

In the first draft of the chapter legalization was discussed. I decided that this topic would only draw attention away from the main intent of the publication. The major issue for me is that a full range of professionals must become involved in the many problems of drug abuse. The arena cannot be left solely to the criminal justice system and drug counselors.

Chapter 10
Suicide

Why Suicide?

It is important to think through some of the explanations for suicide since any response to the problem will depend on how the behavior is viewed. Many contradictory statements have been made over the years regarding the essential nature of the act of suicide. In past years the predominant belief was that it was a crime and/or a sin. This belief prompted such practices as burying the suicide victim with a stake through the heart. This was common at one time in England. There was also a time in the past when a suicide victim was refused burial by the church. In the United States as recently as the 1960s suicide attempts were often treated as something against the law, a "crime" for which a person could receive a jail sentence.

There are many classical arguments around the topic of suicide that attempt to describe the conditions under which it may or may not be an immoral deed. Saint Augustine and others argued that the Sixth Commandment, "Thou shalt not kill," prohibits suicide and that we are bound to obey a Divine commandment.

Strong statements against suicide behavior can be found in the writings of John Locke and Immanuel Kant as quoted below:

> . . . *Men being all the workmanship of one omnipotent and infinitely wise Maker; all the servants of one sovereign Master, sent into the world by His order and about His business; they are His property, whose workmanship they are made to last during His, not one another's pleasure . . . Every one . . . is bound to preserve himself, and not to quit his station willfully.*
> *(John Locke, Two Treatises of Government, Chapter 2)*

We have been placed in this world under certain conditions and for specific purposes. But a suicide opposes the purpose of his Creator; he arrives in the other world as one who has deserted his post; he must be looked upon as a rebel against God. So long as we remember the truth that it is God's intention to preserve life, we are bound to regulate our activities in conformity with it. This duty is upon us until the time comes when God expressly commands us to leave this life. Human beings are sentinels on earth and may not leave their posts until relieved by another beneficent hand.
(Immanuel Kant, Lectures on Ethics, p. 154)

For the purposes of ministry it is critical to validate the worthwhileness and the dignity of life. The Judeo-Christian tradition upholds the eternal consequences of earthly life. Within this tradition we are bound to face life events with faith and hope. But this does not give us license to pass judgment on the behavior of others. A suicide crisis is not the time to ponder moralistic judgments.

Inferences Regarding Cause From Trends and Correlations

As one moves from an analysis of ethical and religious positions on suicide the first step is to look more closely at the types of people who are involved. This can be ultimately helpful in responding to specific crisis events. The statements on suicide rates for particular categories of people in the United States invite inquiry into why given categories should have high or low rates. What is it, for example, about the experiences or problems of the 20- to 24-year-old white male in the United States that increases the possibility of suicide? At the other end of the age scale, why is the white male over 65 years old at high risk? The pattern for the older male is more understandable with the additional information that one particular sub-population of older males is especially at risk. This is the

218

person who has been married and has experienced a good life but then faces serious health problems or loses his wife in death.

There are some interesting observations on the various factors found together with or correlated highly with suicide. Care is needed in the interpretation of these correlations, however. They do not in and of themelves outline a "theory" of suicide behavior. This information does at least suggest that we must take a closer look at how such social systems as the family, formal organizations and society at large are structured in terms of possible impact upon suicide rates. Research in the hospital setting, for example, shows that major staff turmoil is associated with an increase in suicide rates among patients. If a public school becomes embattled or the family is in turmoil then higher rates of suicide can be expected. If adults fight, this can increase the suicide rate for children.

On the national level it would seem that the divorce rate is highly correlated with suicide rates for the 15- to 24-year age category of youth. This should not be interpreted to suggest that children from divorced homes are at extremely high risk. If there is a high divorce rate in the country then some youths are more prone to commit suicide. Another family factor of importance is the number of one-person households. As this rate goes up the suicide rate increases. The absence of a viable extended family system would therefore seem to be important as a factor related to suicide rates. Intuitively, it is tempting to equate suicide with hard times. This would be demonstrated by an increase in suicide during national economic recessions. But the available data suggests an opposite trend. The higher the median family income the higher the suicide rate. As the wealth of a society increases the suicide rate increases. One explanation for this is that during times of affluence the expectations are very high. Under these conditions it is easy to feel that one is not getting a fair share of the wealth. This may produce the kind of stress contributing to suicide.

Theories of Suicide Based on Non-Clinical Experience

Any explanatory scheme can be evaluated in terms of how well it explains suicide behavior and how useful it is for intervention. This book takes a very practical view in relating to problems. But it must be recognized that information that may say very little about what to do in a crisis may, in fact, be valuable in the total understanding of suicide. This applies, for example, to the first major study of suicide as reported by the sociologist Emile Durkheim in 1895. Durkheim saw suicide as a function of how society is structured. He placed emphasis upon conditions such as the degree of integration in a society. He also looked at the amount of regulatory control as expressed by the clarity of norms.

It is not difficult to follow some of Durkheim's thinking on an intuitive level. One might predict suicide in situations where people lack basic social support. We are social by nature and need a sense of being part of society. On the other hand, people can become so intimately identified with society that they lose their unique identity. This can result in the kind of suicide behavior followed by some Japanese pilots in World War II as they deliberately guided their planes into American targets knowing that they would die in the process.

A number of sociological and psychological theories now add to our understanding of suicide in addition to the seminal work of Durkheim. Research has been done on such issues as the relationship between levels of frustration/aggression and suicide rates. Suicide has been correlated with patterns of national economic recessions and periods of strong economic growth. One interesting line of inquiry has called attention to minority status and suicide. Minority status in this research is defined as a condition in which the person does not "fit in." This would include, for example, a white person living in an all-black neighborhood as well as a black person living in an all-white neighborhood or any other combination of minority status.

Some authors who have written about suicide have discussed biological factors. One theory, for example, held that a genetic factor explained a run of suicides in a single family. Studies of twins one of whom had committed suicide found no support for such a factor. Another direction for research using biological factors has been the attempt to isolate biochemical variables related to depression and ultimately to suicide but this research has not produced definitive results.

One of the major problems in the study of suicide has been the lack of solid data. Considerably more work is needed by social scientists. The advantage of basic research is that it can be replicated and theory refined or modified accordingly. I would like to see more interest in the special problems of suicide for the street populations I encounter at night.

Understanding Suicide From a Clinical Perspective

A Psycho-Dynamic Approach

Some professionals working regularly with suicidal patients use approaches based upon a sensitivity to the underlying emotins and self-concepts motivating people. From this perspective, followed for example by Kim Smith, considerable emphasis is placed upon such characteristics of high risk attempters as: the tendency to hold feelings inside, not telling others when one hurts and high expectations of self. Now we are talking about specific factors useful when relating to someone who is at risk for suicide. Dr. Smith helps people express their feelings as one way to reduce the risk. People at high risk for attempting suicide are often individuals who take themselves very seriously. These people expect to achieve, they always work and struggle, getting angry at limits. A particularly high-risk person would be the child in a family with high expectations who does not live up to these expectations.

Another part of the psychological pattern discussed in relation to suicide is the tendency to have high expectations of other people. If others are expected never to make a mistake, the mistakes in real life can be shattering. Adolescents are especially prone to feel hurt when someone lets them down. This may trigger a strong desire to hurt another person in some way. Suicide is one way to hurt someone else. This reaction is especially strong in the case of the loss of a close love relationship in adolescence. Adults seldom understand the intensity of attachments during the teen years. When a boy or girl discovers that a very special love is no longer interested in them this can be truly crushing. One suggestion for parents is to stay in touch with the serious involvements, standing ready to help if a crisis in relationships should develop.

Given the crushing finality of the behavior, it is easy to regard suicide as a single-minded rush to death. But available information suggests that in fact such a person generally has very mixed feelings about ending life. There are thoughts of death but also feelings that death is not something to rush into. The topic becomes a high priority on one hand but on the other hand the person at risk will draw away from an open discussion of it. Some of the best intervention strategies take advantage of the internal conflicts to move the person into a lower risk situation. One such strategy, for example, might be to identify with the person's struggle instead of superimposing all directives from some source external to the person.

Depression can become part of the system of feelings leading to suicide. But depression in itself is not a necessary precursor to suicide. Other factors must be considered including the coping mechanisms used by the individual to manage depression. It is best to consider a pattern of feelings and attitudes, not one isolated emotion. Four factors that together place anyone at greater risk are: 1. The tendency to suppress emotions, 2. High achievement orientation, 3. The inability to release expectations of others and 4. Ambivalent feelings about death.

Suicide is considered when depression turns to hopelessness. In a state of hopelessness that is most traumatic a person senses extreme difficulty in preserving a preferred sense of self and is also caught up in a desire to destroy or hurt a frustrating person or object. From this perspective it becomes important to think about those images that make up a "life fantasy." Life fantasy is a desired state of affairs and defines what sort of person someone is or aspires to be. The more rigid the life style, the higher at risk the person is for suicide.

If someone is in the process of killing himself there is no time for talk about "life fantasy." But most encounters are not that desperate. People need help in thinking through personal aspirations. A major physical loss such as the loss of an arm or leg in an accident can immediately throw a person into panic over the felt inability to be what they dream of being. Most losses I see are not that traumatic but they are vested with considerable emotion by the one in stress. A typical situation, for example, is the felt loss of a loved one who has been taken to jail. All hope for the future may be lost. Recognizing the impact of a shattered life fantasy can be very helpful when confronting specific people.

Most people today who become involved in a helping relationship see the importance of active engagement with the one who is being helped. Suicidal people in particular need more than a passive listener. One specific goal in such a relationship is to build an empathetic bridge between the helper and the one who is being helped. The professional must understand the person's point of view about what is wrong.

A good helper will take time to listen. There must be considerable caution in being too quick to negate all that another says. It is critical to communicate a sense that the person is being heard. Anyone who says simply "Life is not that bad, you have a lot going for you, what's the problem?" is speaking out of an inability to understand.

In the building of an empathetic bridge the first explanation the other gives must be taken seriously. The high school student, for example, may say "I am going to kill myself because I got a B." The exchange must stay with this explanation until the person himself/herself sees the weakness of the statement.

One part of ministry is to share in the task of helping people express feelings. General comments can be made about the tendency for people to hold feelings inside and the potential danger of doing this. There can also be some consideration of what the person wants to accomplish through suicide and/or who the person wants to hurt. This awareness can be helpful for family/friends and others even if they are not active in a counseling capacity with the suicidal person.

A therapist working with life fantasy problems will be interested in exactly how the life fantasy is being threatened. Others close to the patient can be helpful if they are aware of this kind of probing. They, in fact most likely make up part of the troublesome fantasy in some way. In therapy the attempt will be made to help the person see what he/she feels hopeless about. The person may feel hopeless about any number of things including spouse, parents, boy friend, girl friend, school or something or someone else. With a probing into specific areas there can be movement away from the sense that all is hopeless to a more realistic and more manageable awareness of what is apparently hopeless. A good therapist will travel the road with the patient.

While working with a patient the therapist will be aware of key factors that can increase the level of imminent risk. These factors include, 1. Threatened changes in family support, 2. Threatened changes in hospital support if the person is hospitalized and, 3. Events that reduce hope and self-esteem. More will be said about risk factors shortly. Everyone should be aware of those life events that create considerable stress for people. With such awareness it becomes easier to demonstrate support when it is most needed.

In some cases a person who is discharged from a hospital after treatment for suicidal behavior becomes the primary responsibility of a minister or some other professional who is not a suicidologist. In these cases it is helpful to have some awareness of who is at high risk upon release from the hospital. Kim Smith reports the following factors as being of critical importance for pointing to high risk:

Factors That Increase Risk at Hospital Discharge

1. Absence of family or friends in the immediate area.

2. Discharged to live alone.

3. Absence of job or daily and meaningful outpatient structure.

4. Absence of definite appointment for follow-up.

5. Successful treatment of alcoholism.

6. Episodes of rage in an abstaining alcoholic.

7. Negative feelings toward hospital staff.

8. History of serious prior attempts.

9. Tendency to hold feelings in, to become withdrawn and depressed.

10. Increasing pseudo-independence (for example, acts like he can do it on his own, setting up a false facade.)

11. Increasing signs of overt dependency.

12. Recent death of loved one.

13. Reluctance to invest in serious discharge planning.

14. Heightened self-disparagement.

15. Recent disfigurement after major surgery or re-evaluation of a chronic illness.

16. Veteran under 35 with limited resources.

17. Recent recomposition after an extended or severe psychosis. Psychosis is seen as a defense, a regressive defense against dealing with reality in a better way. It can be a gratifying mechanism. The person can he helped to move into a more realistic framework but when this is done the world may seem more hollow to him.

A Behavioristic Approach

In contrast to psycho-dynamic approaches to suicide Marsha Linehan (1981) and many other suicidologists favor some combination of cognitive theories as the best practical background from which to intervene in the case of suicide behavior. From this perspective suicide is seen as a form of problem solving behavior. It is one way to solve stress a person can't handle. Suicidal and non-suicidal people vary primarily in their degree of ability to endure difficult situations and their felt ability to solve problems. Some people are either not able to solve problems or are not willing to solve them. These people find it very difficult to accept the fact that life is a struggle. They think that someone should help them. They refuse to do it on their own. A pattern of living is developed in which life is regarded as not really worth living.

Additional insight is provided by those approaches that describe suicide as a kind of communication. An attempt at suicide is a call for help, a signal that someone is in trouble and needs assistance. When a family member attempts suicide others respond quickly if they are around. Most people do not make more than two suicide attempts. The behavior is a very potent form of communication. But there are always better ways to communicate.

Suicide is problem-solving behavior that communicates something to others. It is basically a form of behavior much like any other form of behavior. All behaviors are influenced by the consequences they trigger. In relating to suicide behaviors, we must consider the perceived consequences of such behavior for the person involved. This is a good place to make a distinction between the ultimate act of suicide and self-inflicted injuries which do not result in death. The latter type of behavior is called parasuicide. Although parasuicide behavior can ultimately end in suicide the two can be considered independently. When someone attempts suicide and gets a great deal of attention in the process this can reinforce the behavior, increasing the likelihood of the same behavior in the future.

Responding to Suicide and Parasuicide as Behaviors

One way to respond is to consider primary prevention or stopping it before it becomes a problem. It is important to call attention to the basic need for an enhancement of interpersonal relationships and general life skills as ways to reduce the risk of suicide.

We can be promoters of more openness in problem solving within the family. Family members need to learn that it is okay to express both "good" and "bad" feelings. In the Christian family we must do more with the celebration of life, with the bold affirmation that there is joy in living. If faith and hope are a natural part of daily life all members of a family should capture some of the positive fall-out. On the downtown streets programs of ministry provide a valuable service by offering the possibility of help in times of crisis so that people can better solve problems or at least see the possibility of solving problems in ways other than resorting to suicide.

Moving away from primary prevention toward actual suicide behavior there is considerable value in reviewing available material on general crisis management. The following list gives 17 specific procedures all of which are valuable practical ways to respond to potential suicide behavior:

Strategies for General Crisis Management
(J. N. Butcher and G. R. Maudal, 1976)

1. Offer emotional support.

227

2. Provide opportunity for catharsis.

3. Communicate hope and optimism.

4. Be interested and actively involved.

5. Listen selectively, respond to workable material and ignore irrelevant or unmanageable aspects of the case.

6. Provide needed factual informtion.

7. Formulate the problem situation.

8. Be emphatic and to the point.

9. Predict future consequences of various plans of action.

10. Give advice and make direct suggestions.

11. Set limits: establish rules.

12. Clarify and reinforce adaptive responses.

13. Confront the client's ideas or behavior directly.

14. Terminate a session abruptly if the client is not at the point of working on his or her problem.

15. Make concrete demands or requirements on the client before the next contact.

16. Work out explicit, time-limited contract.

17. Enlist the aid of others.

Most programs of ministry offer emotional support. This is done by showing an interest in the person, by stopping to listen and by demonstrating some kind of care, understanding and concern. It is also done by avoiding judgmental remarks. Providing opportunity for catharsis means simply letting a person express feelings of guilt, sin, shame or failure. It is not easy to communicate hope and optimism. Pat cliche statements like "everything works out okay in the long run" just do not cut it. An important part of this and any other communication is the covert dimension including body language and feelings given off. These hidden messages may be more powerful than spoken words.

One of the most difficult steps for volunteers in street ministry and for ministers in general is the matter of listening selectively. We do not need to respond to every bit of input. Strangers will "wander around the bush" and/or give us information we can do nothing with. We must make a conscious effort to respond to workable material, procedure number five on the above list. For example, if someone says "I don't know where I can sleep tonight, my mother in Kansas has cancer and I'm afraid of nuclear war" the obvious first step is to talk about available emergency shelters. In other encounters listening selectively becomes much more difficult. The important point is that we can exert some control over the situation, we don't need to encourage a prolonged elaboration of some sex orgy or other items not central to the problem if in fact we are focusing on a given problem. By nature we are all prone to meander over the meadows, we need to be pulled back again and again to the main road.

I will not elaborate on points six through 17 on the list of "general crisis management procedures." These procedures are rarely found in street ministry but are desperately needed. They all say that we must do far more than just listen with caring. Some work is involved, i.e. giving information, predicting the consequences of different plans of action, giving advice and confronting the person's ideas or behavior directly. The latter means that there will be times when we should say something like, "That is an irrational plan at this time." We are part of the process of movement toward wholeness. We do not just listen.

Evaluation of Degree of Risk

One of the most important strategies when dealing with a suicide situation is to evaluate the degree of risk in the situation. The list below contains some 15 factors associated with risk of suicide or parasuicide. It is important to keep these factors in mind. Most of them are general knowledge. The best way to approach the list is to start with the "high danger" factors. If these conditions are present and no one intervenes the person will be dead soon. There is considerable discussion in the literature about the role of alcohol consumption in suicide. Suicide is not a symptom of alcoholism. People do not seem to use alcohol simply as a way to dull their feelings in such situations. It is, however, often found together with serious suicide behavior. Alcohol consumption, therefore, becomes one of the important things to check along with the other high risk factors:

"Factors Associated with Imminent Risk of Suicide or Parasuicide"

(Marsha Linehan)

I. Direct Indices of Imminent Risk for Suicide or Parasuicide:

1. Suicide threats.

2. Suicide planning and/or preparation.

3. Parasuicide in the last year.

4. Suicide ideation.

II. Indirect Indices of Imminent Risk for Suicide or Parasuicide:

5. Client falls in suicide or parasuicide risk population.

6. Recent disruption or loss of interpersonal relationship: Environmental changes in past month.

7. Indifference to or dissatisfaction with therapy.

8. Current hopelessness, anger or both.

9. Recent medical care.

10. Indirect references to own death: arrangements for death.

III. Circumstances associated with suicide and/or parasuicide in the next several hours/days.

11. Alcohol consumption.

12. Suicide note written or in progress.

13. Methods available or easily obtained.

14. Isolation.

15. Precautions against discovery or intervention: deception or concealment about timing, place, etc.

The above list has two primary purposes, first it can be used to estimate the degree of danger at any particular point in time and secondly it can be used to alert us to the kinds of things we need to do to reduce the danger. To reduce the danger we counter the individual risk factors as best we can. For example, in the case of a possible suicide within a matter of hours or days one strategy is to make lethal methods more difficult to obtain. Another strategy is to reduce the social isolation factor.

Moving away from the highest risk factors on the list (those under Number III), the risk factors fall into three main groups, 1. Talk about and preparation for suicide, 2. Recent negative experiences (medical care, loss of relationships, hopelessness, for example) and 3. Relative position within a suicide or parasuicide risk population. The easiest part of this evaluation is the direct talk about suicide. This must be evaluated along with recent losses. With this in mind we must be more alert when people talk about reverses. They may go on about the loss of a job, loss of a family member and other losses but never mention suicide. We may want to probe about how they are coping with these losses. It would be natural here to ask about depression and taking one's own life if the situation points to considerable hopelessness.

The work of Marsha Linehan includes a detailed listing of specific factors defining degree of risk for any one individual. I will not repeat this list in its entirety. The factors she has found to be significant fall into three major categories: 1. Cognitive factors dealing with how the person thinks about his/her world and self, 2. Physiological/affective factors concerned with the body and feelings and, 3. Overt motor behavior including the behavior of having attempted suicide before. If one approaches these factors in terms of trying to improve the situation he will find that hard work will be necessary. If the person is a "poor problem solver," for example, one can help by trying to reinforce improvement in this area. A negative self-concept takes years to develop and may take a long time to change. An interesting difference between the parasuicide and suicide person is that the former is angry about treatment in the past while the latter just doesn't seem to care. This is another situation where hostility may have some value. There are health factors and age factors to watch for plus factors such as alcohol and drug abuse and the status of being unemployed or retired.

To a certain extent good common sense can be used in the evaluation of degree of risk. Some ways to commit suicide, for example, are obviously more of a potential risk than other methods. A gun pointed at the head is more dangerous than poison arrows from a tribe in a jungle the person expects to visit in ten years! But we must be cautious in relying too heavily on "gut level" feeling that someone is at high risk for suicide. It is important to ask specific questions if possible and to think about such factors as indications that someone is making "final" plans, recent losses and coping skills.

It frightens me to think that in the community of faith we may increase risk for suicide by not encouraging an honest confrontation with life problems. We must let people in on the secret that life is not all a bed of roses. There are good days and bad days, good events and bad events. When we sugarcoat everything with spiritual pep pills this may make things more difficult for the person who really "hits the wall." Unfortunately such a person may see failure as a sure sign of sin and this will only add to the problem. We need hope. We also need assertiveness training, experience in coping with the good and the bad, the best and the beast of life. We also need basic information about suicide.

Some Specific Treatment Recommendations

The list below gives some specific treatment recommendations. This is the kind of material one would get if he were taking course work on suicide as part of the training to become a professional in the field. The recommendations must be modified when applied to street ministry work, general pastoral work or the activity of family and friends. Most of us for example, do not carry large caseloads of people at high risk whom we see at regular intervals. But to the extent that we see people on a follow-up basis the suggestions including such details as keeping in possible 24-hour contact can be helpful. We can also use other agencies. The local 24-hour Crisis Line is always a valuable resource.

Some of the recommendations on this list are essential for the work of street ministry. This includes most of the items under "General Considerations." The first three items in particular need our attention: 1. Talk openly and matter-of-factly about suicide. This means not getting all emotional about the topic., 2. Avoid pejorative explanations (the kind of explanation in which we describe the person as weak, for example.) This is just not helpful to the person and 3. Go with a problem-solving theory of suicide behavior, suggesting that it is a maladaptive and/or an ineffective solution to the problem. This means that we must seek out with the person the most positive responses and encourage a pattern of better exploration of options, bringing other people into the act whenever possible.

Suicide Specific Treatment Recommendations
(Marsha Linehan)

I. General Considerations:

1. Talk about suicide openly and matter-of-factly.

2. Avoid pejorative explanations of suicidal behavior or motives.

3. Present problem-solving theory of suicidal behavior and maintain a stance that it (suicide) is a maladaptive and/or ineffective solution.

4. Involve significant others, including other therapists.

5. Schedule sessions often enough and maintain session discipline such that at least some therapy time is devoted to long-term treatment goals.

234

6. Stay aware of the multitude of variables impinging on the client: Avoid omnipotent taking or accepting of responsibility for clients' suicidal behavior.

7. Maintain professional consultation with a colleague.

8. Maintain contact with clients who reject therapy.

II. Pre-Crisis Planning:

9. Anticipate and plan for crisis situations.

10. Continuously assess suicide and parasuicide risk.

11. Be accessible.

12. Utilize emergency/crisis/suicide lines in the area.

13. Give client a crisis card: phone number of therapist.

14. Keep client's phone number and address and phone number(s) of significant other(s) with you.

15. Make a short-term suicide contract and keep it up to date.

16. Contact a client's physician(s) about risk of overprescribing medications.

III. Maintenance of Therapeutic Contingencies for Suicidal and Non-Suicidal Behaviors:

17. Do not require suicidal talk or ideation for client to get your attention.

18. Express caring openly: give non-contingent warmth.

19. Clarify and reinforce non-suicidal responses to problems.

20. Identify probable therapist responses to client suicidal behavior.

21. Confront the client with realistic expectations about other's responses to future suicidal behavior; including suicide.

It is very difficult to work with street people in the area of suicide. Some of these people have learned that they can get attention by trying suicide. This may get them medical attention, for example, when no other way seems to work. A skillful suicidologist would try to make a distinction in these cases between parasuicide and suicide. One way to reduce the risk for these people is to eliminate some of the possible reinforcement. A prominent suicidologist, for example, recently described a situation in which she gave her time to listen to a woman staying in a shelter who talked about cutting her wrist several times in the past. When this woman asked for help the professional told her that the next time she cut herself she should not tell anyone about it. This was intended to break the pattern of reinforcement for the behavior. In street contacts there is little control over the situation. There is a much greater possibility of ending the contact in a way that is not totally satisfying for yourself or the one who is being helped.

On the street I have been more involved with survivors/friends of suicide victims than with people actually moving toward suicide themselves. The act of suicide is one of the most traumatic events for family and friends to confront. We need to pull out our best listening skills. This includes simply repeating what someone says as a way to underline their feelings. We should not judge them in terms of their particular explanation of the event. We can turn to hope and we can be sincere in showing concern. This is a key place for spiritual ministry. But words should not be forced nor sprayed on in a few well-worn cliches.

Survivors may have spoken concerns about the eternal status of the suicide victim. My position is that we are commissioned to comfort the family/friends. I would never lay more pain on them by saying that their loved one is now eternally damned because of the suicide. In the immediate trauma the theological issues are really secondary. We must openly respond to the deep pain. The best funeral service for a suicide victim I have heard of was one in which the pastor giving the eulogy at the graveside broke down and cried with the family.

Legal Issues

As part of the anticipation of becoming involved in a suicide event it is important to become familiar with the legal procedures for suicide behavior peculiar to a given city and state. Specific laws vary from one locality to another in outlining the steps which are to be taken when someone becomes a "danger to themselves." Three issues are involved in legal processing: 1. The actual legal code, 2. The long-range consequences for the client, and 3. The possibility of a malpractice suit against the therapist/minister. In the State of Washington a mental health professional is called upon to determine the need for immediate custody. The relevant sections of the Washington State law are given below to give some idea of what this general type of law includes:

(2) When a mental health professional designated by the county receives information alleging that a person, as the result of a mental disorder, presents an imminent likelihood of serious harm to himself or others, after investigation and evaluation of the specific facts alleged and of the reliability and credibility of the person or persons providing the information if any, the mental health professional may take such person, or cause by oral or written order such person to be taken into emergency custody in an evaluation and treatment facility for not more than seventy-two hours as described in RCW 71:05.180

(3) "A peace officer may take such person or cause such person to be taken into custody and placed in evaluation and treatment facility pursuant to subsection (1) (d) of this section. (From the Revised Code of Washington, Chapter 71:05.180)

The above legal guidelines and similar guidelines for other states say that when a person shows signs of being a danger to himself a designated representative of the city or state can inititate a process ending in forced confinement for a 72 hour period. This can have a number of serious implications for the person including possible loss of a job from failure to report for work. Most 24-hour crisis intervention telephone services operate on the principle that any potentially serious situation should be responded to with strong security measures such as tracing the call, alerting the police and moving the caller toward forced custody.

Is it necessary to force a person into protective custody? This is one of the nagging issues professional therapists must confront. Placing the person in custody will generally prevent the immediate suicide. But the process may alienate the individual to such an extent that he or she will never again seek help or let people know when a potentially lethal act has occured such as the taking of an over-dose of pills. In the best of circumstances a legal hold would be enacted only within the context of considerable familiarity with the situation. A professional therapist working with a person at risk for suicide is more likely to initiate custody procedures as a means of protection against malpractice action than as a part of therapy.

If a minister becomes involved in long-term contacts with a person who is suicidal he/she may need to consider the possibility of malpractice action. But in general, the types of contacts in the ministry including the work of staff and volunteers in downtown ministry are such that there is little danger of legal action if a person does actually kill himself/herself. In recent years, however, there has been a growing tendency for

238

ministers to carry malpractice insurance. When a person enters into a counseling relationship with a professional therapist family members can and do take legal action on occasion when the client commits suicide. There is considerable ambiguity in the legal traditions surrounding such cases. Most court action is based upon an uneven pattern of the outcomes of specific cases instead of carefully defined statutory statements. Professionals carry malpractice insurance and sometimes make decisions based upon the potential for future legal action. The safest procedure is to push the client into tight security whenever a crisis develops. But this may not be in the best long-run interest of the client.

In street ministry we are not in a position to have a great deal of control over the person we see. The issue is seldom one of "forcing" confinement. We can evaluate the situation to the best of our knowledge and act accordingly. Most of the time family and friends follow this same course. Fortunately, it is often possible to get special help from local counseling services if the contacts continue over time. Looking at a wide range of issues is helpful not only for the one at risk but also for anyone who tries to help. It is good to know, for example, that there are limits to intervention and that sometimes long-term counseling may be necessary.

The next chapter turns to the topic of mental illness. One danger in looking at suicide is to see it only as a form of "mental illness." This is a very limited framework for viewing the particular behaviors around suicide. As indicated in this chapter, one reasonable way to consider suicide is to take the position that it is a form of behavior guided like other behaviors by actual or perceived rewards and punishments. The person at risk will not be served well by the one who looks for mental derangement in suicide. Mental illness merits considerable attention on its own.

Summary

This chapter includes a brief over-view of different ways to gain perspective on why people commit suicide together with intervention strategies from the view of the suicidologist. Correlational data is given. This helps by giving insight into those factors often found together with suicide. From a clinical perspective a psycho-dynamic approach is considered with practical implications and a behavioristic view is summarized. This latter base for intervention is given together with specific lists of factors to look for in evaluating risk for suicide and issues in general crisis intervention. The chapter ends with comments about suicide not being just another form of mental illness. The next chapter gives selected material on mental illness with special reference to late-night ministry and ministry in general.

Chapter 11
Mental Illness

Psychotherapy

The term "psychotherapy" refers to more than the work of Freud on psychoanalysis. Many different methods are now used in direct contacts with people who seek out professisonal help including such very different approaches as behavioral modification and milieu therapy. A basic definition of psychotherapy is given below:

> *Psychotherapy is a form of treatment for problems of an emotional nature in which a trained person deliberately establishes a professional relationship with a patient with the object of removing, modifying or retarding existing symptoms, of mediating disturbed patterns of behavior and of promoting growth and development. (Lewis Wolberg, 1954, p. 3)*

As another author indicates, all forms of psychotherapy share the following:

> *1. The patient's explicit or implicit desire for help.*
> *2. An attempt to establish a working relationship with the therapist.*
> *3. An active process which engages the therapist and the patient.*

Over the years there have been major changes in formal responses to chronic mental illness. It is interesting that many of these changes have their origin not in the shifting popularity of given forms of psychotherapy but in such factors as developments in medications and the economic, political and social pressures around mental illness. A major turning point came in 1963 when deinstitutionalization was first promoted.

This has resulted in the proliferation of community mental health centers and a focus on "treatment" in the community instead of in the large traditional state hospitals.

The system responding to mental illness has been slow in adopting the kinds of major changes that deinstitutionalization invites. Most professionals, for example, acknowledge that the system of community life must be given more attention. It is not normally what goes on between a recognized "clinic" or "counselor" and one person who is "mentally ill" but what happens in the total round of contacts and relationships in the city that determines the outcome for any one individual. Many times the most urgent need is for supportive intervention, not deep psychological probing. The situation is a natural challenge for street ministry and other forms of ministry within the church.

> *In any plans for the future new and innovative methods of treatment of the chronic mentally ill must be developed. Any plan must be based on the fact that treatment for many chronically ill patients would be life-long, not limited to 90 days of hospitalization or an arbitrary number of treatments of the current popular therapies. The goal of treatment should be primarily supportive, not at deep psychological levels but geared to helping the patient be as happy and comfortable as their condition permits. This goal will require a wide variety of community agencies to meet different problems in coping with life. Many helping people, such as family members, community volunteers, and consultants from various therapeutic and rehabilitative disciplines, could also be used in the treatment plan. Careful coordination of the different agencies would be necessary to prevent chronic patients from getting lost in the maze of social agencies and bureaucracies. A national health plan could provide the necessary facilities to prevent gaps in treatment or any abrogation of responsibility for the welfare of the chronic mentally ill citizens. (Marion Kalkman and Anne Davis, 1980, p. 6).*

One of the strengths in moving away from traditional, limited office contacts as the condition sine qua non of therapy is that people who do not have extensive training in psychology can in fact be reinforced for positive contacts with others. A professional in the mental health field, for example, gives the following outline of how one might go about helping someone in distress. Sometimes the work of a street minister includes a deliberate follow-through of such steps.

> *"Think, for example, what you would do if a close friend came to you upset and told you he was having trouble with his boss or that he was not getting along with his wife. Probably, you would begin by listening to him. You might ask some questions to clarify your picture of the problem. You would probably show concern and sympathy about his predicament. You might then point out some aspects of the problem that your friend had overlooked and that would tend to place the situation in a different, more hopeful light.*
>
> *You might even suggest to him certain steps that he could take to resolve the difficulty, and finally you would probably indicate that you would like to talk to him again. The second time you saw your friend you would listen to the further developments, perhaps praise him for his effort to resolve the problem, or perhaps you might indicate to him why, on the basis of past performance, he stood a good chance of clearing up his difficulty.*
>
> *You can treat your patient in very much the same way. The essence is to allow him to express himself freely and for you to convey interest, friendliness, encouragement and also a measure of good sense. (—, 1962)*

Reality Therapy

Reality therapy is one example of an approach to people that can be used without going to an in-depth probing of the past. I encourage volunteers in ministry to take the major steps

243

in this model seriously. Reality therapy was first introduced by William Glasser who tested the approach in his work with people having a chronic pattern of mental illness. He reinforces the value of focusing on the present, not the past. Glasser also emphasizes the need to help others become more effective problem solvers. A "friendly counselor" approach to the patient is favored in Reality Therapy. Meaningful, genuine communication is involved. One of the comments of Glasser sometimes overlooked is that at least in the given problem area the therapist (or minister) must be healthier than the patient. The basic principles of Reality Therapy are listed below:

Basic Principles of Reality Therapy

(from William Glasser, *Reality Therapy*, 1965)

1. Be personal — show that you care.

2. Focus on present behavior — not feelings (if patient says "I feel depressed" the Reality Therapist responds with "What are you doing to make yourself depressed?")

3. Focus on the present.

4. Bring in value judgments — each person must judge his own behavior and evaluate what he is doing to contribute to his own failure before he can he helped.

5. Planning — help the person make specific plans to change failure behavior to success behavior.

6. Must have commitment — make and follow through on plans.

7. No excuses — Therapist makes it clear that excuses are unacceptable.

8. Eliminate punishment — eliminate punishment when a person fails — must not make punishing statements like "I knew you couldn't make it."

The above principles are a guide to the major steps in Reality Therapy as summarized below:

The Major Steps in Reality Therapy

1. Find out what the behavior is we are trying to correct.

2. Must accept reality — cannot rewrite a person's history.

3. Must make it clear to person that past events are not to be used as an excuse for behavior which is irresponsible.

4. Person must take full responsibility for what is happening to him now.

5. The basic need for all is need for an identity — need to feel separate and distinct from every other person and must have meaning associated with this identity.

6. The approach is for daily living — not just for the mentally ill.

7. This approach does not give labels to mentally ill but sees mental disturbance as irresponsibility. Does not focus on the past — does not focus on the unconscious.

A Customer Approach to Patienthood

This modeled is proposed by Anne Burgees and Aaron Lazare. The approach sounds overly simplistic. But it can be an important adjunct to the work of ministry. The basic idea is that a key element in getting help to a person is knowing what the person wants. This demands familiarity with the person and taking time to understand needs. One of the ways Jesus worked with people was to ask them what they wanted from him.

One step in using the customer approach is to categorize the kinds of requests coming to an agency or program of ministry. In a clinic patients want many things, from simple information about the clinic to advocacy type intervention. Sometimes clinicians try so hard to understand deep, underlying problems that they ignore the obvious. One example of this is the case of a man who seemed very depressed. Counselors were undecided about how to proceed until he was asked what he wished they would do. He said he wanted his wife to be moved so she would be on the hospital ward where he worked so that he could see her more often. When the transfer of the wife was accomplished the husband's depression disappeared. Not every case is this simple but it does illustrate the advantage of stopping to probe the wishes of the person who is being helped.

After reading the article on a customer approach I did a study of the kinds of requests coming to the volunteers in Seattle's late-night ministry. I reviewed all of the nightly log reports for a two week period. The requests during that time could all be placed under one of the following categories:

Requests Coming to One Late-Night Ministry

1. Request for directions, advice or physical help.

2. Expressed desire for conversation/social contact.

3. Inquiries around a specific spiritual need.

4. Request for money.

5. Solicitation for coffee or food.

246

6. Seeking lodging for the night.

Given the people served by this program on the downtown streets late at night one might expect a high percentage of requests for money. But this was not the case. Money, coffee and/or food were not the most popular things to demand. Conversation, social contact and directions were the most popular focus for requests. There were only six specific requests for spiritual help out of a total of 68 requests. Two of the requests for social contact turned into exchanges around spiritual need.

It would seem logical that a person with a pressing physical problem would want to have some satisfaction that this problem was going to be met before wanting to pursue problems around an emotional or spiritual need. This follows the adage that it is difficult to preach to a man when he is starving. The danger in this assumption is in thinking that once the meeting of basic physical need is assured such as the need for a night's lodging, the person will then be eager to talk about higher order needs. The data from this study do not support such a view. There would seem to be some people who are interested in specific spiritual needs and others who want food or shelter. One possibility is that a person might want food or lodging one night and then want to consider spiritual needs some other night. It would seem to be unrealistic to push every encounter into a discussion of religious issues.

When asked to indicate whether the request came during the first few minutes of a contact, after the conversation had gone on for several minutes or at the end of the contact there was a strong tendency to indicate that all requests came early in the contact during the first few minutes of a conversation. This lends additional support to the notion that there is often a separation of requests instead of a process of starting with the most elementary and building to higher issues.

In a program of late-night ministry one would anticipate that there would be a fairly equal distribution of requests for spiritual services among the Protestant pastors, Roman

247

Catholic priests and Roman Catholic sisters working on the streets and in the taverns of the city. Based on the limited information from this study of requests this assumption is not warranted. The spiritual requests come overwhelmingly to those in the Seattle program who are older (over 50) and who have been in the program longer (one year or more). This invites inquiry into the special characteristics of these people who receive most of the requests for spiritual help. People on the street and in the taverns apparently make a fairly quick assessment and early in a contact begin to focus their request. Some clergy invite spiritual requests by their mannerisms, their speech or their familiarity with the people and places of the night scene. Others are more likely to receive the pleas for food and lodging without a balancing of requests for spiritual counsel. One of the obvious implications of this is that serious attention must be given to the need for retaining people in the program as well as to the recruiting of new volunteers.

There are many ways to use a greater sensitivity to requests in the general work of the church. One possibility is to tabulate the kinds of requests coming to a local church together with a listing of those people in the church who respond to requests. One of the more general values of a request orientation is that it places the focus upon the person who is being served. There is always a danger in allowing a contact to become primarily an opportunity to elaborate upon opinions and/or judgments without stopping to inquire what another person may wish. As suggested by clinicians using the customer approach to patienthood, the approach calls attention to basic philosophy regarding patient and professional. In the case of lower social classes there may be considerable disparity between the goals and expectations of the patients and the therapists who treat them. Lower class patients, for example, often expect the therapist to be warm and directive while the clinician may expect to be nondirective and neutral. The customer approach breaks through such an impasse in expectations. There are similar kinds of diaparities in the contacts between parishioners and professionals in the church.

Discussion

The material in this short chapter must be placed in context with the discussion given in Chapter 6. It is important to reaffirm the reality that many people become involved in the process of what might in general be called "counseling." Some pastors have extensive training in the process of intervention with dysfunctional behavior. Given the long history of people seeking special help either from a minister or from a church counseling agency it is surprising to find reluctance on the part of some parishioners to use professional guidance. One barrier is the notion that if one just tries harder to be a good Christian everything will be okay.

Reality Therapy as introduced in this chapter is now a dated approach and overly simplistic for in-depth counseling over time with patients. But I like some of the guidelines in this approach as shared in the preceding pages. In street ministry the time has come to be part of the move toward wholeness, not becoming just another band-aid. This can call for straight talk encouraging others to gain as much control as possible over their situation. At times, however, this is not the way to proceed since the demand is for totally supportive input.

I would be interested in more work on a "Customer Model" of helping within the Church. This could start with an analysis of how Jesus often first wanted to know what he could do for someone. In ministry we must be pulled back again and again to the real hurting person.

One of the serendipitous outcomes of this chapter and of the book as a whole is that street or downtown late-night ministry takes on a new look. It becomes apparent that such work can become very demanding, confronting many different kinds of problems. This is the kind of uncertain situation promoting new frontiers of ministry. Hopefully this book will serve along with other works coming out on similar topics to inspire new levels of service both in the parish and out on the streets of the city.

References

Becker, Howard
1963 — *Outsiders, Studies in the Sociology of Deviance*, New York, Free Press.

Brownfield, Rod
1980 — "Being There," *Ministries*, September, p. 9.

Burgess, Ann W. and Aaron Lazare
1976 — *Community Mental Health: Target Populations*. Englewood Cliffs, New Jersey Prentice Hall, Inc.

Butcher, J. N. and G. R. Maudal
1976 - "Crisis Interactions" in I. B. Weiner (Ed.), *Clinical Methods in Psychology*, New York, John Wiley.

DeQuincey, Thomas
1907 — *The Confessions of an English Opium Eater*, New York, E.P. Dutton and Company.

Durkheim, Emile
1897/1951 — *Suicide, A Study of Sociology*, translated by J. A. Spaulding and G. Simpson, New York, Free Press.

Flaubert, Gustave
1979 — *Madame Bovary*, a new translation by Mildred Marmor, New York, New American Library.

Glasser, William
1965 — *Reality Therapy: A New Approach to Psychiatry*, New York, Harper and Row.

Glatt, Max M.
1974 — *A Guide to Addiction and Its Treatment*, New York, Halstead Press.

Golding, William
1954 — *Lord of the Flies*, New York, Coward-McCann.

Jellineck, E.M.
1960 — *The Disease Concept of Alcoholism*, New Haven, Ct. College and University Press.

Kant, Immanuel
1963 — *Lectures on Ethics*, Translated by L. Infield, New York, Harper and Row.

Kalkman, Marion E. and Anne J. Davis
1980 — *New Dimensions in Mental Health Psychiatric Nursing.* New York, McGraw-Hill Book Company.

Keller, John
1966 — *Ministering to Alcoholics*, Minneapolis, Augsburg Publishing House.

King, Warren
1982 — "Schizophrenia, the harrowing madness," *The Seattle Times*, April 26, pp. B1 and B5.

Kozol, Jonathan
1988 — *Rachel and Her Children: Homeless Families in America*, New York, Crown Publishers.

Lieber, James
1986 — "Coping with cocaine," *The Atlantic*, January, pp. 39-48.

Linehan, M. M.
1981 — "A social-behavioral analysis of suicide and parasuicide: Inplications for clinical assessments and treatment," in H. Glaezer and J. F. Clarkin, eds. *Depression: Behavioral and Directive Intervention Strategies*, New York, Garland Press, p. 229-294.

Locke, John
1965 — *Two Treatises of Government*, A critical edition with an introduction and apparatus critic by Peter Laslett, New York, New American Library.

Maeder, Thomas
1989 — "Wounded healers, *The Atlantic*, January, pp. 37-47.

Maynard, Steve
1989— "Preacher's son," *Morning News Tribune*, Tacoma, Washington, Sunday, February 26, pp. D1 and D2.

Peele, Stanton
1990 — "Second thoughts about a gene for alcoholism," *Atlantic Monthly*, August, pp. 52-58.

Ratcliff, Kathryn Struther and Janet Bogdan
1988 — "Unemployed Women: When Social Support is not Supportive."
Social Problems, 35:1, Feb. pp. 54-63.

Rudgers, Joann Ellison
1982 — "Schizophrenia," *The Sunday Denver Post,* September 12, pp.
24-25.

Royce, James E.
1981 — *Alcohol Problems and Alcoholism*, New York, The Free Press.

Satir, Virginia
1964 — *Conjoint Family Therapy*, Palo Alto, California, Science and Behavior Books.

Segal, Steven P., Jim Baumohl and Elsie Johnson
1977 — "Falling through the cracks: mental disorder and social margin in
a young vagrant population." *Social Problems*, 24: pp. 387-400.

Smith, Kim
1982 — "Characteristics of patients who suicide in and out of the hospital," Paper presented at "Suicide: Issues in Assessment and Treatment,"
Topeka, Kansas, June 3.

Spradley, James
1970 — *You Owe Yourself a Drunk*, Boston, Little Brown and Company.

Spradley, James P. and Brenda J. Mann
1975 — *The Cocktail Waitress: Woman's Work in a Man's World*, New
York, John Wiley and Sons, Inc.

Spring, Beth
1989 — "Home, Sweet Home," *Christianity Today*, April 21, pp. 15-20.

Van Houten, Mark E.
1988 — *God's Inner-City Address: Crossing the Boundary*, Grand Rapids,
Michigan, Zondervan Publishing House.

Wear, Norma
1987 — Seminar on post traumatic stress and ministry, Tacoma, Washington.

Wolberg, Lewis R.
1954 — *The Technique of Psychotherapy*, New York, Grune and Stratton.

1989 — Revised Code of Washington, 70.96A.020

1989 — Revised Code of Washington, 71.05.180

1962 — "20-minute hour therapy," *Factor*, September included in Riess-man, Frank, (ed.) *Mental Health of the poor: New Treatment Approaches for Low Income People,* New York, Free Press, 1964, pp. 429-430.

"The 12 Steps of AA," Reprinted with permission of Alcoholics Anonymous World Services, Inc. Permission does not mean that AA has reviewed or approved the contents of this publication, nor that AA agrees with the views expressed herein. AA is a program of recovery from alcoholism. Use of the Twelve Steps in connection with programs and activities which are patterned after AA but which address other problems does not imply otherwise.

"Early Warning Signs" Taken from a publication of the National Council on Alcoholism. Reprinted courtesy of the National Council on Alcoholism and Drug Dependence. For a copy of the NCADD "Self Test," please write to NCADD, 12 West 21 Street, New York, NY 10010 and include a self-addressed stamped envelope with your request.

. . . .

The mailing address for the Tacoma Operation Nightwatch program is P.O. Box 1181, Tacoma, Washington 98401. Seattle's Operation Nightwatch can be contacted at P.O. Box 21181, Seattle, Washington 98111.

DATE DUE